100 Ways
to Save and Grow
Your Money

Financial Fitness for Regular People

By Peter Sorrells

BestBooks
LLC

100 Ways to Save and Grow *Your* Money:
Financial Fitness for Regular People

Copyright © 2009 by Peter Sorrells, Gilbert, Arizona

Scripture taken from the HOLY BIBLE, NEW INTERNATIONAL VERSION. Copyright © 1973, 1978, 1984 International Bible Society. Used by permission of Zondervan Bible Publishers.

ISBN: **978-0-9843414-0-5**

Editors: Steve Gobbell, Peter Sorrells
Interior design and cover design: Peter Sorrells
Interior illustrations copyright © 2009 Jupiterimages Corporation.
Cover photography: copyright © 2009 Peter Sorrells
Printed in the United States by Lightning Source www.lightningsource.com

Published by Best Books, LLC, Gilbert, Arizona.
e-mail: manager@BestBooksLLC.com

This book is dedicated to my favorite woman in the world—
my wife, Lori,
who has gone through the fire of financial disaster
and the climb back toward financial freedom with me.
And to our three sons, who have blessed our lives tremendously.
I love you, guys.

Acknowledgements

Big thanks to:

My parents Arnold and Patsy, who taught me about God, Jesus, faith, integrity, compassion, hard work, discipline, making a dollar stretch, and never giving up.

The multitalented Steve Gobbell for his expert editing and ideas, without which this book would be so much less.

Grammy award winner Mel Brown for his inspiration, example, and gracious instruction in publishing. www.fromzerotosideman.com

James Bilodeau for his article "The Simple Steps for Starting Your Own Publishing Company, and Marketing Your Own Book—Masters of Our Own Destiny."

Toby Estler and Jack Kelly for their encouragement, wisdom, and coaching.

Brian Tracy and Steve Chandler, whose teaching and example helped me to prioritize, organize, and complete this project.

All the folks at Lightning Source, who helped transform this project from an idea into a reality.

So many friends and family for listening, praying, and encouraging me to keep moving forward.

Congratulations!

Picking up this book is a great step toward improving your financial future. Its suggestions will help you to put money in your pocket and your bank account, and to prosper like you've only imagined before. You will learn that *you* are in control of that future, more than anyone else. The book is for regular people like you and me; we do not need special skills, extraordinary luck, rich friends, or any money to get started. No matter your history or present financial challenges, you can start right where you are and create a better future.

This book has ten chapters, and each one has ten ideas within that topic. It also has a bonus chapter at the end, with ten more ideas! You may choose one that interests you in particular, and study only that topic. But you will get more benefit from reading through the entire book and then reviewing the topics most interesting to you. This is a reference tool that you can use again and again for the rest of your life, adding new ideas to your own money-growing plan whenever you want. You'll find space for notes at the end of each chapter so you can easily make this your personal notebook and maximize its usefulness. As you read each chapter, your own creativity will spark new ideas. Write them down!

There are so many ideas presented that you will not be able to remember them all at the same time, and you would not want to do them all the first week. It is better to try the two or three ideas that are most appealing to you, make the most sense to you, or apply most to your own needs. Once you have consistently used those ideas and created new habits, you can add another and then another.

Keep track of your progress by measuring your savings account growth (or debt shrinkage, as the case may be) once every two or three months. This will help to keep you motivated to try new ideas, stay disciplined, and grow your money. Measuring much more often may be discouraging, because at times growth can be slower than we like. But waiting more than three months between checks can allow your plan to get out of control and may not provide you with enough feedback to stay motivated and consistent.

Note 1: All the ideas contained in this publication may not be suitable for everyone's particular financial life. They are *ways* a person can increase income, save money, and grow wealth, but every idea may not be right for you. You must consider carefully any change in your financial or tax strategies. Your decisions must conform to the law and must make sense for *you*. Because every individual's circumstances are different, no warranty or guarantee is expressed or implied as to the suitability or effectiveness of any part of this book to a particular person's needs. These decisions are personal ones and require an intimate knowledge of your own finances.

Note 2: This book is distributed and sold with the understanding that neither the author nor the publisher is engaged in rendering legal, accounting, tax, or other professional service. If legal advice or other expert assistance is needed, the services of a competent professional should be sought.

Note 3: This book will help you. Tell three friends about it! It will help them too.

"For I know the plans I have for you," declares the Lord, "plans to prosper you and not to harm you, plans to give you hope and a future." —Jeremiah 29:11

TABLE OF CONTENTS

Chapter   **Page**

Introduction

Define Your *Why*

Before diving into the one hundred ways, it is worthwhile and necessary to discover exactly *why* you want to increase your personal wealth. Why is your own *why* important? Because to save and grow your money, you must change the way you think.

The way you have thought until now has gotten you the surplus or lack of money that you have now.

You will also need some effort and discipline because a human being will only do what he or she wants to do. Discipline does not usually fall into the category of "what I want to do." Therefore you must have a driving reason, a picture in your mind, that is so important that it tugs at your emotions. Your own vision of the future will happen if you apply the principles of success correctly. Here are some reasons to create personal wealth.

1. Money is good, in the hands of good people.

Money is a tool, just as a hammer and screwdriver are tools. One person uses a hammer to build a house; another may use the same hammer to tear down a building, destroy property, or even harm people. Deuteronomy 8:18 tells us, *"Remember the LORD your God, for it is He who gives you the ability to produce wealth, and so confirms His covenant."* You may argue that He wrote this specifically to the nation of Israel four thousand years ago. But even if that is the case, the verse tells us something of God's nature. Being perfect, God does not contradict Himself. Would He therefore create in us the ability and desire to produce wealth, and then ask us not to use it? As with all His gifts, we must use wealth properly.

Most hospitals, advances in medicine, churches and charities that clothe, feed, and otherwise minister to the world would not be here today without the generous gifts of those who had first created wealth. A lot of the progress made against poverty and HIV/AIDS in the world has been made because of the generous donations of those who have some money to give—not only by governments.

According to the Hudson Institute at www.global-prosperity.org, the Index of Global Philanthropy shows that 75 percent of the developing world's economic dealings with developed countries, comes from private donations. The report goes on to say that *"private philanthropy and remittances that migrants sent back to families in their home towns constituted four and one-half times U.S. official aid abroad"* (Hudson Institute, May 12, 2008).

Money has gotten a bad reputation during the past century and that reputation is just wrong. The founders of our country were wealthy and gave all that wealth to birth a new nation—an entirely new form of government. Many heroes of the Bible were blessed with material wealth: Abraham, King David, and Job. Even the wealthy Greek Christians are mentioned by the apostle Paul as they donated to help the persecuted believers in Jerusalem.

It is true that some people have gotten their money unethically or used their money for evil purposes. But money is a magnifier of your character and values; good character and values result in ethical creation of wealth and using that money for good causes. If we search the Scriptures, we can understand the source and reasons for wealth. Many have misquoted 1 Timothy 6:10 to say, "Money is the root of all evil," when in fact it says, "The *love* of money is a root of all kinds of evil" (emphasis added). Loving people and using your money to help and bless them, is a noble way to live—not so different from God's own generosity toward us.

You have to get over the mistaken idea that it is somehow wrong to think, plan, and work to build a store of money. Even to build it large enough to protect your family, launch charities, and bless others. What did Jesus, the Son of God, do from age 12 to age 30? He worked as a carpenter, and probably not for free. Somebody paid him for his work.

What did He do with the money? He probably paid for his family's living expenses and gave some away to help others. I believe He also saved and grew some of that money. Why do I think that? *"Jesus grew in wisdom and stature, and in favor with God and men."*—Luke 2:52. He was *wise*. And He somehow financed a three-year ministry ahead of time.

I'm not saying He was wealthy, as a carpenter without power tools in a small, poor town. But we are told in scripture that Jesus and His disciples carried their money with them during most of that ministry. They carried a money bag, bought food, and paid taxes while they were changing the world.

2. Your family needs it.

None of us can predict the future. Most of us carry insurance on our homes, insurance on our cars, and insurance on our lives. Yet the overwhelming majority of Americans have no "insurance" on their source of income. Income from a job is inherently risky; any change in the employer's business or the employee's ability to perform can result in zero income for a short or extended period of time.

Which one of your family members does not deserve protection in the unfortunate event of losing your regular paycheck? Any employer can downsize or "right-size," but it all boils down to one thing: loss of income for someone—you or someone you care about. Building a nest egg of liquid cash and diversified sources of income can make the loss of your employment a minor irritation rather than a major catastrophe.

3. You want the good life.

Have you and your spouse ever fought because there was too much money in your checking account? The argument is usually because of the opposite: too much month left at the end of the money. There are loved ones to visit, sights to see, history to live, boats and planes to ride, braces to put on your children's teeth, cars to drive, beautiful homes to live in, college for each child, parents to care for. And that trip to Hawaii or Europe that you promised right before you were married. Almost everything you have dreamed of doing in your lifetime that has not happened, has not happened because of a lack of money or a lack of time, both of which a surplus of money would fix. Through the proper approaches and a little discipline, you can eliminate one of the most common sources of stress in marriage. Define together, in detail, what you want to achieve in spiritual growth, finance, marriage, parenting, travel, and lifestyle. Then...

Save and grow your money.

"Humility and the fear of the LORD
bring wealth and honor and life."—Proverbs 22:4

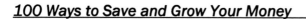

Chapter 1

PLASTIC ATTACK

"The borrower is servant to the lender."—Proverbs 22:7b

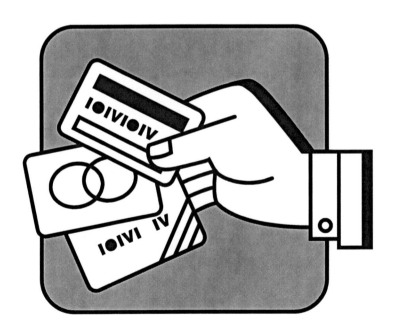

Credit cards have probably caused more grief for more families than any other single entity. They are so easy to use and so hard to pay off. And because we live in a society that values instant gratification, we buy almost *everything* on credit rather than waiting until we can afford to buy with cash. If you have fallen into this trap, don't feel bad, and don't feel alone. Banks and stores spend millions of dollars in research and advertising to separate you from your money. But you *can* get out of the trap. This chapter is dedicated to that freedom, and the first recommendation is this: stop using credit cards except for emergencies and when needed to rent cars and hotels. It is too easy to run up a bill that is larger than you can pay at the end of the month. Once you do that, you'll be giving money to the bank in the form of interest payments for as long as it takes to pay off the card.

1. Credit card monthly balances

Train yourself to pay off credit card balances in full at the end of the month. This will prevent you from building up a balance (and monthly payment) that you can't afford. Any month that you do not pay the balance in full makes the next month more difficult to pay (assuming you charge more the following month). Each successive month becomes more difficult to pay off, and it becomes a runaway train that you can't catch. This is how people get into trouble, borrowing from one card to make a payment on another card, which is impossible to sustain in the long run. You have to go after the principal balance (the amount you owe). If you already have a large balance that you think you can never pay off, read on, and take courage. I have been there. The constant worry and stress can be exhausting; but you can use those strong emotions to shape and empower your new actions and habits. Those new actions and habits will reverse the trend from sliding deeper in debt each month to climbing upward each month. You will dig out of this hole.

2. Credit card interest rates

Take a good look at your most recent credit card statement, and see what percentage of the payment went toward the principal (the amount you owe) and how much was purely for the finance charge. If you haven't done this before, you'd better sit down first. And maybe bite on a bullet.

Call all of your credit card companies (the telephone number is on the back of the card), and ask for their lowest interest rate. They will often give you a lower rate just for asking! I didn't believe it, but I tried this at the advice of a friend, and every single credit company reduced my rates. If you have kept your payments current, it is not unusual for the bank to reduce your rate from as high as 25 percent to as low as 8 percent.

It's sort of like prayer. James 4:2b-3 says,

"You do not have, because you do not ask God. When you ask, you do not receive, because you ask with wrong motives, that you may spend what you get on your own pleasures."

So ask God; He is keenly interested in this area of your life, as He is interested in all areas of your life. Then ask the bank for a lower rate. The banks are certainly not God, but they do have control over your interest rate and they *will* reduce it if you ask. This can make a huge difference in monthly payments, and the portion of that payment that will go toward paying off the balance. As a result, you'll be paying off the debt faster.

Here is an example using a $5,000 balance, assuming you want to pay it off in two years. You can see that reducing the rate makes the payment smaller. But changing from 25 percent to 8 percent interest can save almost a thousand dollars during the two years you are paying off the card:

Rate	Monthly Payment	12 Months of Payments	Savings in 2 Years by Reducing Rate
25%	$267	$3,202	
18%	$250	$2,995	$414
13%	$238	$2,853	$700
8%	$226	$2,714	$977

3. Consolidation

Then consolidate some of the higher-rate balances onto lower-rate cards to shrink your overall payments and reduce the payoff time. Important: Do *not* spend this money, or change your lifestyle. Instead, apply the money you'll save in interest payments each month toward the principal balance (the amount you owe) on the *lowest-balance, highest-rate* card. Keep doing that until that card has a zero balance. There is no better feeling than writing "paid in full" in the memo of the last check to that credit card company.

Then attack the next-lowest balance, next-highest rate card, and so on. The progress you'll make in one year will surprise you.

Remember, don't use the slight increase in available cash each month to buy more stuff. Credit cards are a ball and chain around the neck of your family's finances and future. The only way to cut it loose is to take out your hacksaw and dedicate yourself to the goal of cutting through the chain. That means applying all newly available cash toward erasing debt.

4. Minimum payments

If you have only one credit card and cannot pay the balance in full at the end of the month, always pay more than the minimum payment. In fact, always pay as much as you can possibly afford that month. It can take five years or longer to pay off a credit card if you are only making the minimum payment. Some financial websites say it can take up to *22 years*. Unless you attack the principal balance (the total amount that you owe) aggressively, you will pay thousands of extra dollars in finance charges. You can use some of the other ideas presented in this book to come up with more cash to apply toward the principal on your cards. If you will attack the principal every month, with all the cash you can afford, you will be able to free yourself from the ball and chain and start working to live rather than living to work.

The following table shows that you can save a lot by paying more than the minimum payment. This example uses a $5,000 balance and $150 minimum monthly payment. If you make no other new charges and your interest rate is 18 percent, it will take nearly 4 years to pay off the balance. But increasing the minimum payment by $100 a month (total $250 payment) reduces the payoff time from four years to two years, saving $1,200 in interest charges. That's cash back into your own pocket.

In the 25 percent interest example, increasing the minimum payment by $116 (total $267 monthly) reduces payoff time from five years to two years, saving 3 years and $2,600 in interest charges! *Your* hard-earned cash.

Interest Rate	Minimum Payment	Time to Payoff	2-year Payoff Payment	Time Savings	Cash Savings
25%	$150	5 years	$267	3 years	$2,600
18%	$150	4 years	$250	2 years	$1,200

In that same 25 percent example, your $150 minimum payments would total $9,000 in five years. Yes, you will pay nearly twice the credit card balance, if you only make minimum payments and the interest rate is large. It's better to attack the balance and pay more than the minimum every month so that you can wipe it out fast.

You can find easy-to-use calculators for credit cards and other debts at this Web site: www.walletpop.com/calculators.

5. Savings vs. high-interest debt

It doesn't make sense to earn only 3 percent on your savings account while you are paying 18 percent to 25 percent to a credit company. Taken together you are still losing money every month, to the tune of 15 percent to 21 percent. You are getting further into debt rather than building wealth. So make debt eradication your most immediate goal. Keep enough money in the bank for emergencies, and use the rest to wipe out your debts. Then you'll be able to grow your savings much faster because the monthly credit card payments will be *gone.*

How much cash is enough for emergencies? That number is probably different for everyone. $100 is way too little and $10,000 is out of reach for most of us, at least in the beginning. A nice round number like $1,000 sure can reduce your stress and help to pay the unexpected medical bill or car repair. Using some of the techniques outlined in this book, you can build that up pretty fast just $10 at a time.

6. How many cards?

After paying credit card balances down, force yourself to live with only one or two credit cards. Cancel the other accounts to avoid temptation and annual fees. Once you have built a good track record with a particular bank or other financial institution, you can usually qualify for a great line of credit on a single card. Another side benefit here: if you lose your wallet or purse, only one or two cards will be at risk. Most credit cards protect you for any fraudulent charges over $50.^{00} if you report the card stolen right away. If you owned six credit cards, your liability would be $50 × 6 = $300. Fifty dollars is better.

One more benefit: If you do have to make phone calls to report a lost or stolen card, then waiting on hold for an hour with two banks is better than waiting on hold with six banks.

7. Impulse buying

Never use credit cards for impulse buying. If you don't have the money to buy the item with cash, you probably won't pay off the credit card balance at the end of the month either. Usually these are not emergencies. Rather, an expensive advertising promotion or well-trained salesperson has convinced you that you've *got to have* this thing. But it's only a thing. Your family's financial security, freedom, mental and physical health must take a higher priority. Nothing has ever been sold that won't be for sale again later when you have the cash!

8. Cash advances and fees

Never use credit cards to borrow cash. The interest rate is astronomically high, and the creditors charge you that interest from day one. When you buy something with a credit card, however, they do not charge interest until the closing date of the statement. Emergencies are another story, but let's stick to a strict definition of the word *emergency*. A purse on sale is not an emergency! Anything on sale is not an emergency. Your child needing immediate medical care—that's an emergency. Your car needs repair so that you can get to work—that's an emergency. Cash used for any purpose other than an emergency should be cash that you have already saved for that specific purpose. Planning and discipline are the foundation on which you must build your family's finances.

If you happen to make a late payment, your credit card bank will immediately charge a late fee (according to www.creditcards.com, they'll charge $20.5 *billion* in penalties this year). If you accidentally go over your limit, they will also charge you an overlimit fee (maybe $39 or more). If you do both at the same time, you could be adding $70 or more in fees to your debt every month. If this happens, call your credit card bank (the phone number is on the statement and on the card), and explain what happened. For example, you were out of town, had an unexpected medical bill, or your car broke down and you had to fix it to get to work. Then ask them to remove those fees as a courtesy. If you have been paying

14

on time and keeping your balance under the limit most of the time, they will back these fees out for you—one time. That may be enough to bring your balance back under the limit. You can make your payment that day over the phone using your checking account or debit card, and you'll be a hero to the credit card company. You can use that opportunity to ask for a lower rate too.

9. Building your credit rating

Do use credit cards to build a credit rating, but only after planning carefully. Only charge as much as you can afford to pay in full at the end of the month, and then pay off the balance in one lump sum to avoid interest charges. In this way you can build up a history of regularly paying off debt. This technique is useful if you have never had credit before or have gone through a bankruptcy or foreclosure and need to rebuild your credit rating. For example, buy your gasoline with a credit card, and pay the full balance at the end of the month. The better your credit rating, the lower interest rate you can get on your credit cards, car loans, and mortgage for your house. The monthly savings can be from tens to hundreds of dollars, depending on the size of your balance. Mortgage payments can differ by $500 a month or more, just by qualifying for a lower rate!

10. Cash vs. plastic

Plan your spending carefully, and save your money until you can afford to buy with cash. Planning for automobiles, furniture, education, and even household repairs will make the buying event much more enjoyable and stress-free. If you have already saved money for a specific purpose, there will be no "buyer's remorse."

There will be no worrying about how to make the payments on a new ball and chain. Once you have paid off all your credit cards, saving for any goal will be easier because the money you formerly paid in interest every month will be going into your savings account. Your savings will grow *fast* when you have a positive cash flow.

You may even want to try an envelope system for a few months or a year, to help you plan and prevent more debt. The best way to do this is to hide your credit cards. Give them to a trusted family member, or bury them in a coffee can in your back yard. (If you're like me, you can just put them in a safe place inside the house, and within a week you won't remember where they are.) Then label about twenty envelopes with each category of your spending plan.

Put cash in the envelopes from each paycheck, according to the amount you expect to need for that category (such as food, gasoline, entertainment, rent or mortgage, electricity, clothing, car payment, haircuts, credit card payment, phone, internet service,). It's like a budget that forces you to color inside the lines. Once an envelope is empty, you can't spend any more in that category. And you won't be able to increase your debt because you aren't using your credit cards.

This system makes discipline easy, and builds good habits for any budgeting system you may use in the future. Make sure to have an envelope for savings, and don't pull anything out of it except to make a deposit at the bank.

NOTES

Chapter 2

GIVE YOURSELF A RAISE

*"She sees that her trading is profitable,
and her lamp does not go out at night."*
—Proverbs 31:18

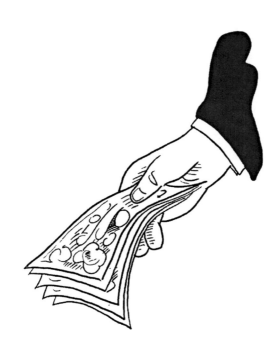

1. Pay yourself first.

Have you ever felt like you are working only to support the bank, the water company, and the landlord, because there is no money left at the end of the month? This chapter will help you pay *yourself*, to see the benefits of your own labor in your own bank account and your own standard of living. First and most important, put a portion of each paycheck into a savings account that you never touch, no matter how tight that week or month may be. We humans are adaptable creatures; you will learn to live on what's left of your income. If your employer were to cut your rate of pay suddenly, you would have no choice but to live on a smaller amount, yes? In fact, before your last raise, you did live on that lower income, didn't you?

I have traveled in several Asian countries and have many friends in that part of the world. I have learned first-hand that most individuals in that culture save more than 50 percent of their income, every month. They live on less than half of their paycheck, on purpose.

Therefore, from your own experience and from the example set by our friends in Asia, we know it is possible. As your salary or wage grows each year, increase the percentage of income that goes to savings each month. A good target is 10 percent. I will prove it to you later in this book, but a person saving 10 percent of his or her income steadily for 40 years can be a millionaire at retirement, unworried about the future of Social Security.

If you can't manage 10 percent, start with *something*—even if it is only 1 percent in the beginning.

2. Savings accounts

After wiping out high-interest debts, put a fixed percentage of each paycheck into an emergency fund and a fixed percentage into a "fun fund" to save for that new TV, sofa, ATV, guitar, or vacation. Set a definite goal first (both the amount and the date you will have it), and then calculate the amount you will need to deposit each month. The numbers don't lie. If you don't save a definite amount regularly toward a definite goal, the only alternative for any expense is your old enemy: the credit card. Putting money into your savings account every month is "paying yourself" rather than paying the bank. In a savings account or Certificate of Deposit (CD), *the bank pays you* for the use of your money. What a concept!

3. Interest rates you pay

Shop around for the best interest rates on credit cards, automobile loans, home mortgages, and other debts that you have not yet paid off. Interest rates vary widely among banks, credit unions, and other institutions. One place you can search for the best deals is www.bankrate.com. You can save *big* dollars every month just by refinancing higher-interest loans or transferring balances into lower-interest products. After reducing the payments, *use the extra money each month to build wealth.* What will it feel like when you can see a whole year of salary sitting in your checking account? It might feel *free*—at least, worry free.

Only a small percentage of Americans will ever see that, because they lack information, or discipline, or both. But anyone can have that cushion—including you—by using the principles and truths in this book.

Truth. Let that sink in for a moment. Jesus Christ said, *"You will know the truth, and the truth will set you free"* (John 8:32). He was talking about His truth: who He is and what He came to do for us—to die for the forgiveness of all our sin. But His statement is true of all truth. If you have the correct knowledge (truth about how money works) and apply some discipline to what you have learned, you will eventually become financially free. Jesus came so that we would be free from the law of sin and death; I can't do that for you, only He can. But if you'll do what I am teaching in this book, you will become financially free.

4. Interest rates you receive

Shop around for the best interest rates on your savings account too. Every bank offers different savings programs and rates, and you do not have to keep your savings account at the same bank as your checking account. You may even find some online, but make sure they are FDIC insured. (The FDIC is a government agency that guarantees your principal will not evaporate, even if the bank fails.) CDs can pay more than passbook savings accounts but usually require a minimum deposit and may tie up your money for six months to five years. Build a foundation of liquid cash of several months' income in case of emergency before putting cash into long-term investments that have withdrawal penalties.

5. Interest on checking accounts

Find an interest-bearing checking account, and never keep a checking account that charges you a monthly fee for the use of your money! A harmless-looking $7.50 monthly service charge is costing you $7.50 × 12 months = $90 every year. In ten years, you will have given the bank more than $900 (plus the interest you *didn't* earn on that money). Moving money to a new account at a new bank is easy. And you might even get a free toaster, DVD player, or extra cash deposit out of the deal. I once had my money at a bank that charged a monthly service fee twice the amount of interest they were paying me. I am so smart that it took me more than a year to figure out what they were doing and close that account. Look at your bank statement today, and move accounts tomorrow if you are getting a bad deal. You'll have to leave some money in the existing account until all checks clear, but you can move the rest of your money to a new bank with zero notice. The new bank will give you a book of new checks to begin using right away.

Your current bank may also have a different flavor of checking account. You may be able to change that type simply by asking, and thereby stop all those fees immediately. A bank representative can usually look at the number of checks you are writing and your average balance, to recommend the best account for you.

6. Transportation

Try carpooling, bicycling, or other forms of transportation to and from work a couple of times a week. If you can save just $5.^{00} a week in gasoline for a year, you've just paid for $260 worth of Christmas or birthday gifts. Or contributed $260 toward your children's college fund or your retirement fund. Or bought a plane ticket for your vacation. Check out these Web sites to find the lowest prices for gasoline in your area:

www.gasbuddy.com
www.gasprices.mapquest.com
www.autos.msn.com/everyday/gasstationsbeta.aspx

The range of prices will surprise you; they can differ by up to 20 cents a gallon in the same neighborhood. If you can save just 10 cents a gallon and you typically fill up a 13-gallon tank every week, you'll put $70 back into your pocket each year. Own a truck or SUV? At 20 gallons filled up six times a month, 10 cents lower on each gallon saves you $144.00 every year. Put a $100 bill and a $50 bill in your wallet and keep them there to remind you.

7. The Jar = paying yourself

Pay yourself $1.^{00} every day. Aren't you worth $1.^{00} a day? Of course you are. Well then...pay yourself! Just take $1.^{00} out of your purse or wallet and put it into a jar—*every day*. After two or three weeks, it will be a habit and you won't even miss that little green piece of paper. Consider The Jar a toll for walking through your kitchen! After doing this for a year you'll have $365 in The Jar to do with as you please. You can spend it on Christmas gifts for the people you love. Or put it into a savings account to earn interest. Or pay off a credit card!

Does $365 sound too small? Do you have $365 in your wallet right this minute? If you had fed The Jar every day for the past year, you would have that money now. If you will make this one simple action into a habit, you'll repay yourself for the cost of this book many times over. Yes? Yes. By this time next month!

My children have used The Jar, so I know you can use The Jar. I remember one of my sons wanting a particular handheld electronic game. He taped a picture of the game onto a jar and then started putting his allowance, birthday money, loose change he found in the sofas—all into The Jar. He even asked for extra chores for bonus allowance. Whenever he was tempted to spend his money on an action figure or ice cream or other junk, he'd look at that picture on The Jar. He saved up enough money to pay cash for that game. This was more than 15 years ago, but I remember that it cost well over $50. He saved all that money a penny here and a dollar there, in about six months. He learned discipline and goal-setting and spending less than he earned—what most adults do not practice about saving and growing money.

He was five years old.

Another time, he and his brother saved for a common goal using the same jar. This time he was ten years old, and his brother was five. They were equally successful achieving their goal as a partnership—using The Jar.

Try this one: put $1.^{00} in the first day, $2.^{00} the second day, $4.^{00} the third day, $8.^{00} the fourth day, and so on, doubling your deposit to The Jar each day. If you do the math, you will learn an important lesson about compound interest and the rate at which savings (or debt) can grow! Of course, this example uses a 100 percent daily interest rate which *would* be great if we could find it, but the idea is the same. Hint: not many people could afford their own deposits by the third week of this program!

Hmmmm...what if you put your daily coffee or cola money into The Jar instead of loading up on caffeine? At $5.^{00} a day, The Jar would pay you $1,825 in *one year*. I love The Jar. You will too.

8. Impulse items

Never buy anything that is hanging at the checkout counter of a supermarket or department store. These are called "impulse items" because people buy them on impulse! You did not plan to buy these items, and chances are they will end up in your junk drawer anyway. If you really needed them, you would have written them on your grocery list, and they would already be in your shopping cart. Multiply $5.^{00} by the number of times you visit the grocery store every week, by 52 weeks, to calculate your true savings. Twice a week at $5.^{00} each is $520 a year that you could have paid yourself.

9. Pay on time.

Pay your monthly installments and other bills on time to avoid late charges. Most automobile loans and credit cards, for example, add about $35 to any payment that is more than a few days late. Not only will you save the $35 every month, your final payment at the end of the loan will be smaller because less interest will accrue. Even if your lender offers a "grace period" for late payments, they are charging you interest for every nanosecond the payment isn't in their hands. Why pay more interest than you have to? If you are a person who routinely pays late charges, even on one credit card, that is costing you more than $400 every year. You could have paid yourself instead. This is another lesson in discipline: put the due dates on your calendar or a PDA that will beep to remind you, so that you will pay on time every month. Or set up an online payment that debits your account on the due date each month automatically.

10. Forgetful savings

Write yourself a check every month when you sit down to pay bills, just as if you were paying any other financial debt (like your electric bill or car payment). Put the check in an envelope, address it to yourself, and drop it in the mail. In a few days you will have forgotten about it, and suddenly it will appear in your mailbox. Those are happy surprises (finding money we had forgotten about)! Enjoy the moment, holding some extra money in your hand, and then deposit it in your savings account so that you won't spend it!

NOTES

Chapter 3

TAX MINIMIZATION

"This is also why you pay taxes, for the authorities are God's servants, who give their full time to governing. Give everyone what you owe him: If you owe taxes, pay taxes; if revenue, then revenue; if respect, then respect; if honor, then honor."
—Romans 13:6–7

Share these ideas with your tax accountant or financial advisor. Of course, any tax strategy must be legal, and must be correct for your own financial circumstances. Always seek the advice of a professional before changing your tax plans.

1. Assess the damage.

Right away, before doing anything else, look at your last two tax returns—not just the refund due line or the amount due lines at the bottom of page 2. Look a little higher on page 2 at the *Total Tax*, about line 60. This is what you actually paid in taxes. Most of it was withheld from your paycheck, and you never saw it, but it is (was) your money. For a lot of people, this number is about a fourth of their gross income. A big number for all of us. The more you can reduce that number, the faster you'll wipe out debt and build wealth for your family. Knowing the number gives you fuel for motivation and discipline—to change the number.

2. Home ownership

If you do not already own your home, you should consider buying one when your financial condition allows. In some parts of the country, rent is only a little smaller than a mortgage payment. In that case, you have little to lose and a lot to gain by owning rather than renting. Where I live, mortgage payments can be double the average rent, but it still makes sense to buy a home whose monthly payment is appropriate for your income. Of course there are closing costs and a down payment to consider. But if you are planning to stay in one place for several years, consider this: renting for $1,000 a month, you will spend $12,000 every year out-of-pocket, and own nothing.

But owning a home with similar payment, the interest deduction will net you about $1,000 in tax savings. That tax refund can go toward debt elimination or wealth creation; and the house itself will appreciate (increase in value) most years, which will deliver wealth over time (see Chapter 7, Around the House, for more information).

And paying a mortgage instead of rent, you are shrinking the debt a little bit every month. Eventually you can own the home free and clear, with no house payment or rent to pay. That frees up $1,000 every month for fun, helping others, giving to causes that you care about, living expenses, whatever you prefer.

3. Tax deductions and tax credits

Take every legal deduction and tax credit for which you qualify. Tax deductions are subtracted from your reported income before calculating the tax owed. That means that a tax-deductible expense will reduce your tax burden by the tax rate multiplied by the deduction. In other words, if your income puts you in a 20 percent tax bracket, then a $100 tax deductible expense may net $20 in reduction of your tax (added to your refund or subtracted from what you owe).

Tax credits are different. They are subtracted directly from the tax owed—dollar for dollar. No matter what your tax rate is, a $100 tax credit nets $100 in reduction of your tax (tax you do not have to pay). A $1,000 tax credit nets $1,000 in tax savings.

There are federal credits and state credits that vary depending where you live. For example, in Arizona there are school credits enabling you to donate money to a school and then to receive a 100 percent credit back on your taxes. The donated money buys books or new uniforms or playground equipment for the school, and you get 100 percent of the money back at tax time.

	Tax savings at 15% tax rate	Tax savings at 20% tax rate	Tax savings at 30% tax rate
$100 Tax Deduction	$15	$20	$30
$100 Tax Credit	$100	$100	$100
$1,000 Tax Deduction	$150	$200	$300
$1,000 Tax Credit	$1,000	$1,000	$1,000

Everyone has a duty to pay taxes, but there is no sense paying more than the law requires. Your tax advisor can help here; you can also learn about tax deductions by using a software program like TurboTax® to prepare your return. Tax laws change every year, so make sure to get information and software for the current tax year.

4. Optimize allowances.

Look at your last two tax returns again. Did you receive a large tax refund after filing? Some people like to get that big check in April, but think again. The IRS had the use of your money for more than a year. They started withholding taxes in January of the year before, and then sent you a refund in April of the next year. They had some of your money for sixteen months! That was your money the whole time, but you could not use it to wipe out credit cards or even to help pay bills or avoid late fees.

You can be further ahead by reducing your withholding rate and using your money to pay down debt and build savings, every month. Earn interest instead of letting the IRS hold your money. You'll have to discipline yourself to use that money for reaching your goals—not more spending. It's easy to change your withholding rate: ask your employer for a new W-4 form, and claim more withholding exemptions. How many? There's an easy calculation in the W-4 instructions to help you figure that out. You can also get these forms online at www.irs.gov.

This simple change can net you a hundred dollars or more every month—more than receiving a modest raise in pay. Applied to a payment on a 23 percent credit card, this can mean a finance charge savings of more than $200 a year and faster payoff of the entire debt.

5. Receipts are critical.

Keep receipts for *everything,* and log them into a spreadsheet or accounting program such as Quicken® or Quickbooks® for easier tabulation at tax time. This includes donating $10 to a coworker for a Cancer Climb. Most people don't have to endure an IRS audit, but if you do, you'll be glad you have the receipts. They are hard evidence of your deductions. If you keep the receipts in a safe-deposit box for protecting tax records, you can even deduct the cost of the safe-deposit box.

Note: If you are thinking that it's too much trouble to track these receipts and expenses, remember the example of The Jar. If this exercise controls even $5.^{00} of tax-deductible expenses every few days, it gives you hundreds of dollars in potential tax refunds.

6. Charitable giving

Give a portion of your income to charity: medical research, your church, world hunger relief—whatever draws your heart. There are many reputable organizations whose purpose is the saving and clothing and healing and feeding of human beings. You'll save tax dollars for sure—and you'll feel great knowing that part of your hard-earned cash is helping someone who desperately needs it. One great model is the 10-10-80 plan: save 10 percent, give away 10 percent to church and/or charity, and live on 80 percent of your income.

Proverbs 11:24-25 says,

"One man gives freely, yet gains even more; another withholds unduly, but comes to poverty. A generous man will prosper; he who refreshes others will himself be refreshed."

Cool.

It has been said that we cannot outgive God. To those who are financially rich, Paul says in 1 Timothy 6:17-18:

"Command those who are rich in this world not to be arrogant nor to put their hope in wealth, which is so uncertain; but to put their hope in God, who richly provides us with everything for our enjoyment. Command them to do good, to be rich in good deeds, and to be generous and willing to share."

Let's create enough wealth to bless and save lots of other people. Yes? Yes.

7. Small business

Start a small business out of your home. Start with what you have, not with borrowed money, unless you know you can pay it back within a reasonable amount of time. There are more tax advantages for small business entities than for humans. Part of your cell phone, car, travel, tools, office equipment, and other expenses may be deductible to the extent they are used for business (check current tax laws). Keep all receipts and keep diligent, detailed records of *everything*. See chapter 6 for more information on home businesses.

8. College

Do you hope to send your children to college? Then change your thinking from *hoping* to *planning!* Start saving now, but make sure you have a tax-exempt savings program. Otherwise, you may find yourself earning 6 percent on money that has already cost you 25 percent in taxes. U.S. savings bonds are one route: if used for educational purposes, the interest they earn is usually tax-deductible and in every case tax-deferred. There are also Roth IRA plans specifically for education, which earn tax-free interest.

9. Professional help

Shop around for the right tax accountant. Yes, you can use TurboTax® or a similar program to prepare your tax returns as an individual. But once you begin to hold real estate or own a schedule C business, an LLC (Limited Liability Company), or a small corporation, you should have a professional go through your books and prepare the forms for you. Some companies pay tax-preparers only to fill out the forms for you; these individuals are not financial experts and probably not qualified to give advice tailored to your needs and goals. Make sure to find someone who is knowledgeable, honest, willing to carefully evaluate your business structure, debt load, tax strategy and goals, and to give you some valid advice. Ask for references!

10. Truth, the whole truth, nothing but the truth

Never, ever lie on your tax return. You will only be asking for trouble—and a fine—both of which will cost you money. Because the tax code is so enormous and changes so often (every single year), a good tax accountant or tax attorney will eventually become necessary, as your tax returns become more complex. It is worth having a knowledgeable tax preparer help with your tax forms, or at least to use a program like TurboTax, to help prevent mistakes. Mail or e-file your tax return on time to avoid fines!

NOTES

_____

_____

_____

_____

_____

_____

_____

_____

_____

_____

_____

_____

_____

Chapter 4

INCOME MAXIMIZATION

"Lazy hands make a man poor,
but diligent hands bring wealth."
—Proverbs 10:4

1. Activity

This chapter will give you some ways to increase the flow of money into your hands. If you work an eight-hour shift every day and then sit in front of the TV the rest of the night, chances are that you will be in the same financial state for the rest of your life. Making a difference in your life requires spending some energy on the part you want to change! It also means a little work, discipline, and time commitment. Losing ten pounds to improve your health involves getting off the sofa to exercise. Losing debt and increasing wealth also require getting off the sofa! First, stop watching television—or at least limit your viewing time. Not only does TV cost you time; it also trains your brain to be passive. You must be an active thinker to increase your income!

2. Schedule time for money.

Spend your extra time doing something productive. This doesn't mean that hobbies and family time are bad; in fact, you need them to be healthy. You must be a whole person! Organize your time to create an *average* of seven hours each week to apply toward *your* financial freedom. That's one hour a day, on the average, or an hour every other day plus a half day Saturday. You are giving your boss forty hours or more; giving yourself just seven hours a week will make a huge difference in your financial future.

3. Second job

One way to increase your income is to work a second, part-time job—temporarily. A second job with a local business doesn't have to be glamorous or high-paying. A few hundred extra dollars every month can make a big difference in your program. Restaurant, newspaper company, department store, secretarial agency—the list is endless. It will wear you out, but it is worthwhile for a *short*, predetermined period of time—if you discipline yourself. You must put every penny of the extra income into your savings and investment program or use it to wipe out your debts. Then go back to a single job to keep the rest of your life in balance! Do *not* use any of this money to expand your lifestyle, or you will get onto a never-ending treadmill.

4. Do your best to strive for excellence.

Do your best every single day on the job. There is a definite link between attitude, hard work, and success in income maximization. Try surprising your boss with above-average work and a cheerful attitude. The effect on your position and salary may surprise you. Some studies suggest that the average person may only spend 50 percent to 80 percent of his or her time doing productive work. The rest of the time is wasted talking to coworkers, surfing the Internet, getting ready to work, or getting ready to leave for lunch. Then talking on the phone, e-mailing friends, going to the rest room, texting, and then getting ready to leave for the day. Be different.

If someone comes into your office to chat, you can say hello but then politely control the conversation by asking a question: "Do you mind if we set an appointment to talk about this? I have to finish a project right now." Then stand up and begin to leave. The other person will stand up, too, and the event will be over.

Another strategy that I use to focus my time on completing an assigned project or goal, is to book a conference room or a study room at the library—just for me. I make an appointment with me and my laptop computer, right there on my calendar, for two hours of uninterrupted time. Nobody will disturb me, I won't hear the phone ring, and I can concentrate on finishing the task.

5. Insure your income.

Make sure that you have enough health insurance and disability insurance. You may say that you can't afford it; I say you can't afford *not* to have it. All it takes is one medium-sized health challenge in one family member to wipe out all of your savings and even put you into massive debt. You and your family may be very healthy now; but ask anyone who has been diagnosed with cancer, or who has broken a leg, or who was seriously injured in a crash. Or ask anyone whose child suffers with leukemia or asthma or autism. An uninsured medical condition can take all you've got and put you into a financial hole for years. Better to adjust your other living expenses so that you can buy both medical and disability insurance.

6. Volunteer.

Volunteer for extra training or duties with your employer, that are interesting to you, that you can perform, and that would increase your value to the company. This can lead to more visibility to management, more job satisfaction, and eventually more income. Teaching classes, leading teams, or even volunteering to be a member of a problem-solving team are just a few assignments that have worked for others.

7. Extra cash for showing up

If you work for a company that offers cash awards or incentives for suggestions, patent applications, or article contributions, engage in those programs! With no risk on your part and everything to gain, why not? You could be earning some extra cash by investing a little time to fill out the paperwork. Good suggestions and patents also help to make your company more profitable, which can benefit you indirectly through job security, profit-sharing programs, and bonuses. Use the extra cash wisely (to pay off debt and build savings).

8. Alternative transportation

Some companies offer cash incentives for carpooling or walking to work two or three days a week. If you can take part in a plan like this, you will gain not only the cash incentive but also the money you save in gasoline, oil, and auto repairs. A cash incentive of $10.^{00} a month plus gasoline savings of $5.^{00} a week adds up to $360 a year! ($5.^{00} per week × 4 = $20.^{00} monthly. $20.^{00} + $10.^{00} = $30.^{00} monthly. $30.^{00} × 12 months = $360.) What will you do with that $360? Plan it, and follow your plan.

9. Education and training

Another way to grow your income is to increase your education or training. This can help you to qualify for a higher-paying job at your current place of employment or at a new one. Your employer may provide the training, or you may choose to take courses at a community college or trade school, or even a degree program at a university. It is never too late, and all the education that you gain can make you more useful, more knowledgeable, and more marketable. Many employers will give you time off work to attend classes that are relevant to your job or the next level in your career path and may even reimburse your tuition cost.

10. Ask for a raise.

Don't be afraid to ask for a raise if your work is superior. If the quality and quantity of your work is excellent, and performance reviews are positive, then your employer should reward and motivate you with regular increases in pay. There may be caveats such as financial issues in your company (it's a bad time to ask for a raise during layoffs or just after missing a quarter's goal), but otherwise, there is no harm in asking. My superiors actually told me in one of these conversations, "We didn't know that you wanted a promotion." No kidding, they said it with a straight face. The Scripture is true: *"you do not have, because you do not ask...."*

NOTES

Chapter 5

LIFESTYLE EQUALIZATION

"Whoever loves discipline loves knowledge..."—Proverbs 12:1a
"He who ignores discipline comes to poverty..."—Proverbs 13:18

1. Spend less than you earn.

The long-term effectiveness of all the ideas presented in this book depends on lifestyle equalization. No one who spends every dime of income (or more!) will ever achieve financial freedom or grow a basic savings account. Therefore, all of us have to spend less than we earn. That means using some sort of budget—making a list of all our known expenses, plus a margin for unexpected expenses, at the beginning of each month. Then we must keep track of everything spent in each category. It sounds like a lot of work, but it takes only a few minutes each evening or an hour at the end of the week. Sweating out the bills every month, a result of nonexistent or improper budgeting, ultimately takes a lot more time and creates a lot more stress. See the basic budget form in the back of this book. You may make as many copies as you want, or you may wish to buy a budgeting book. Even better, use a software program such as Excel® or Quicken®—just do it.

If you don't believe this is true—that simply spending less than you earn can make you wealthy and that the opposite will make you poor—consider two polar opposite cases. As I make the final edits of this book, the TV news is announcing a popular performer's sudden and tragic death at the age of 50. He was brilliantly talented and worth about $1 billion in his thirties but plagued by financial trouble and heavily in debt at the end of his life. It is almost a universal behavior that people will spend as much or more than their income unless they learn to take positive steps to avoid that trap, as you are doing now by reading this book.

A person can be broke at any level—and a person with small income can become a millionaire. The amount of income doesn't make as much difference as lifestyle equalization. I recently heard the true story of a pastor of a very small church who never earned more than about $20,000 per year. He retired a millionaire because he saved money from each paycheck, invested it wisely, and never touched his investments no matter what.

2. Discipline

Discipline is critical to No. 1 above. If we are to reach any goal, whether it is an educational goal, harmony in the family, financial success, physical fitness, anything worthwhile, then discipline is not optional. If your financial life has not been disciplined up to now, this may seem overwhelming at first. No problem, just pick two or three simple ideas in this book and do only those. You will be able to look back in three months, six months, and twelve months to see great progress in the form of smaller debt or more money in the bank. Write it on your calendar right now, or program your phone or computer now with an alarm three months into the future. Review your progress quarterly, and then choose the next two or three ideas to start.

Specifically, discipline here means the following:

- Prepare your budget faithfully at the beginning of each month. Note the important word: "your." *Your* budget will help to save and grow *your* money. Nobody else is going to do it for you. And you must remember not to compare yourself to your friends, neighbors, or relatives. They are as far into debt as you, and most have no financial plan to survive a job loss or medical emergency or to prepare for growing old.

- Enter expenses and income *as they occur.* I have let them go for a month or more in the past, and believe me, it's not fun trying to reconcile two or three months of receipts and checks with your checking account. Letting things go can also result in your checking balance falling below zero, and your bank charging large fees for non-sufficient funds. Once—recently, I am embarrassed to admit—I wasn't paying close attention, and nine little checks hit my bank the day before my paycheck was deposited. Nine $35.^{00} NSF charges, far more than the dollar amount of the checks themselves. That $315 in fees—in one day!—wiped out my savings program for the month. A hard lesson learned. Better to keep close track of checks, debits, and balances.

- Pay yourself first! Make a habit of putting a percentage (or fixed amount, as with an installment payment) into your savings account every single month. Enter it into the budget just as any other payment, and do this as surely as you pay your electric bill.

- *Don't touch your savings* just because that cool new toy—an MP4 player or laptop or DVD or *those* shoes—went on sale. There are only two reasons to touch savings: (1) a true emergency that you have no other way of paying or (2) moving the money into a higher-yielding investment.

3. Impulse buying

Impulse buying must stop. Plan your spending carefully; and never buy from door-to-door salespeople unless you find yourself in one of these situations:

- It is an item you were planning to buy already. (Be honest with yourself! If it is not on your goal sheet or a shopping list, then you have not planned it.)

- The money is in your budget for that month.

- The price is lower than you would have paid at the store or online.

4. Junk mail

Don't buy from advertisements sent to you in the mail, unless they meet the three tests in No. 3 above. These ads will offer attractive terms ("only 12.95 per month!" "Cancel anytime!"). But consider this: Add up that $12.95 every month for 12 months. The total is $155, and right now you are realizing why you don't have $155 in your wallet. Most bothersome are the ones that send you a product every month automatically. They know that you will keep the product and pay the money rather than going to the post office to return the item. Cancel that DVD membership now. Use the savings to erase debt and *grow your money*.

5. Cars

What kind of car do you drive? Did you buy it new? Have you ever added up what you are paying for the loan, insurance, taxes, registration, and maintenance? We have to look at those details to understand whether we are living a lifestyle that our income cannot support. And even if our lifestyle seems OK compared to our income, our lifestyle may not be compatible with our long-term financial goals. This is not a suggestion to get rid of a reliable car in exchange for a piece of junk that is also a safety hazard! But if you are driving a new $28,000 car, think about driving a new $15,000 car instead. It still has the "new-car smell" and the reliability of a warranty but will save you more than a thousand dollars a year in payments. Plus there's the difference in insurance cost, registration fees, and so on. That means *a savings of about twenty thousand dollars* ($20,000) over the five-year life of the loan ($13,000 in purchase cost alone and the other $7,000 savings in finance charges, insurance, property tax and registration fees).

If you had done this with your last car five years ago, what could you be doing with an extra $20,000 today? What if you do this for the next five years and put that $20,000 into an investment paying you 5 percent or 10 percent for the next 10 years after that? This one change alone could set up your retirement as a millionaire, or at least a several-hundred-thousand-aire.

6. Used vs. new

If you *must* have that $28,000 car to keep breathing, think about buying that same $28,000 car one or two years later as a used car with 12,000 miles on it, for $20,000. There is always some risk in buying a used car, but if you are careful, you can save big money this way. Most new cars depreciate (lose value) the second you drive them off the dealer's lot. Before you even get the car home, it is worth less than you paid for it. Buying a car *after* this most severe time of depreciation flattens the depreciation curve and saves a lot of your money. Either way, you are driving the same car. One wealthy person that I know always drives a Lexus, but he always buys it two years old.

7. Lunches

If you have been buying your lunch every day on the job, at a cafeteria or restaurant, try brown-bagging it one or two days a week. That is, make your lunch at home and bring it to work. Of course, if you lunch with clients every day, this may be impossible. But if you can do this, it will be another step toward making your lifestyle equal your financial strategy. You can bring a sandwich and a drink from home for about $1.^{00}, instead of $5.^{00} to $15.^{00} for a cafeteria or restaurant meal. Using the minimum amounts, saving $5.^{00} twice a week is $500 a year! Think about it. You may feel that those lunches are worth $5.^{00} to $15.^{00} to you. Are they worth $500? Are they worth $1,500? That's what they are costing you.

8. Outsmart your budget.

While preparing your monthly budget (there's that word again—just repeat, "I love my budget; it saves and grows my money"), keep lifestyle equalization in mind. Think about each amount and whether you could live with even 10 percent less. If you budgeted $500 for groceries, could you do it for $450? Just for this month? And put that $50 into The Jar? Do you need to budget $200 for clothes this month, or could you live with $180 and put $20 against a credit card? If you can cut back any one category, or several categories—even a little—your budget will save and grow your money. Dollars you save in any category can be put into savings or debt elimination.

9. Christmas account

If the Christmas season typically leaves you two or three (or twelve) months in debt, then you must equalize your lifestyle diligently during the holidays. One way to avoid paying all that interest for the gifts you couldn't afford (but bought anyway on your credit card) is to open a "Christmas Club account" with your employer's credit union. (If this is not available, you can open a separate savings or checking account with your bank for this purpose). That way you can deposit small amounts of money throughout the year (which, of course, you plan and budget for each month) and *earn* interest instead of paying it. If you allow yourself to spend only what you have saved for the occasion, you will put money into *your* pocket instead of the bank's pocket.

Many banks will let you program a transfer once or twice every month from your checking to savings account, which happens automatically forever until you tell them to stop. This service can help to build your own Christmas Club account.

10. Serial buying

Serial buying rather than parallel buying can help you save money and earn extra interest on your deposits. Banks, insurance companies, and your employer understand this concept well, and use it to their advantage. The longer you can avoid paying, the more interest you will earn on the money left in your account. Use this technique when shopping: buy only what you can reasonably use rather than stocking up on items you might need in two or three weeks.

Buying everything at once has these results:

- More food will spoil before you have a chance to eat it.

- You will buy some things that you will never use.

- You lose the interest that you could have earned if the money had remained in your account for another month.

Buying serially has these results:

- You will buy only what you need.

- You will find it easier to meet your budget.

- You will earn more interest on your money because more of it will stay in your account!

- Or, you can use the money you would have spent on next month's groceries, to pay down a credit card this month.

If you shop at discount clubs, be careful to check prices compared to sale or coupon prices at your grocery store. Some items at the discount club are a great discount; others are not. The sizes can be huge on some products, which may spoil or expire before you use them. This waste may erase the savings that you achieved by buying at the discount club. Here we find again the importance of discipline and planning. Plan before leaving home, buy only what you need, and buy only what is on your list.

The exceptions to serial buying are discount buying in bulk when you are sure you will use the products, buying items on sale, and buying with coupons. If the items are nonperishable or can be frozen, then it might make sense to buy ahead at a discount. Another test is whether you need to use that money for a credit card payment or other debt to reduce finance charges or avoid late fees. Within reason, the more items you buy on sale and stock in your freezer or pantry, the more money you'll save. Don't go crazy with this and overstock or buy things you will never use. Buying early only saves money if you replace a higher-cost future purchase with a lower-cost purchase today.

NOTES

_____

_____

_____

_____

_____

_____

_____

_____

_____

_____

_____

_____

_____

_____

Chapter 6

MIND YOUR OWN BUSINESS

"Make it your ambition to lead a quiet life, to mind your own business and to work with your hands, just as we told you, so that your daily life may win the respect of outsiders and so that you will not be dependent on anybody."
—1 Thessalonians 4:11–12

1. Keeping up with the Joneses

"Mind your own business" has a double meaning. First, it means to stop comparing yourself (cars, toys, spending habits, appearance, goals) with everyone around you. Keeping up with the Joneses will keep you in financial bondage—just like they are. Start using the proper techniques to maximize and grow *your* money, regardless of what everyone else does.

The average American household is living paycheck-to-paycheck and spending everything it earns – maybe even ten percent *more* than its income. According to the US Department of Labor in April 2009, as reported by www.visualeconomics.com, the average income in the USA is $63,091 before taxes and average expenditures for those households is $49,638. In 2009, IRS taxes for $63,091 are about $11,959 (10 percent of the amount up to $8,350 plus 15 percent of the amount up to $33,950 plus 25 percent of the amount up to $63,091):

Average Income	$63,091
Average Expenditures	-$49,638
Average Tax	-$11,959
Balance (annual)	**$1,494**

That leaves just over $100 a month for savings, charity or emergencies—not much. Any (small) event like a medical bill, legal bill, car repair, or slight change in gas prices will eat that up fast. Little league dues and equipment, or violin lessons, will do it too.

According to spendonlife.com, the average American household has more than $8,000 in credit card debt, so we're actually spending *more* than we earn. And consumer debt grows every year, so debt payments are increasing. This is wealth shrinkage, not growth.

We must dare to be *not* average.

2. Your own business

Next consider starting and running your own business. There are a hundred different small businesses you could choose. In fact, many are available online today that were not available even ten years ago. We will list only a few here to start you thinking. The advantages are many. You can earn extra income. You may be able to reduce some of your income taxes. Some of your possessions and expenses become tax deductible to the extent used for business (car, computer, fax machine, and mobile phone, for example).

Start with what you have. Borrowing money to start a business from scratch can get you into trouble. If you do borrow money for this purpose, it will be "good debt" compared to TVs, vacations, or other depreciating items, which would be "bad debt." But debt is debt, and you have to pay it back. So be careful and be sure about what you are doing. Don't borrow more than you have to, and watch your pennies. You don't want to put yourself into a deeper debt problem than you already have. A more conservative approach, building the business from the inside out, slowly and carefully, is safer and will build a more stable environment. Before investing in any business, make sure to research its advantages and disadvantages thoroughly, meet with people who are already successful in that industry, and ask lots of questions.

Be sure to keep your business accounts and personal accounts completely separate. Open a checking account and credit card in the name of your business, and never, ever use them for a single personal expense. Shop around for your business account. Don't automatically assume it should be at the same bank with your personal accounts. Every bank has different fee structures and check costs; my business bank gave the first order of business checks for free (this can save up to $100 on checks alone).

3. Your computer spits out money.

There are many small businesses you can start with only a small initial investment. You may not have thought about some of them because they don't sound like a business. Let's begin with a simple one: If you own a computer, you can start a typing or data-entry service with the computer you already own. With some training, you can even transcribe medical records or do phone sales or customer service calls using your computer and a dedicated telephone line. Contact local businesses and offer to handle overflow typing or rush jobs.

Our economy has increasingly become a service economy. If you produce superior work, deliver on time, and treat your customers with respect and friendliness, your business will begin to grow. This small typing business probably won't put you in a Ferrari, but if it earns even $100 a month for you, that's $1,200 a year. Word-processing rates are about $15.^{00} an hour, so we are talking about six or seven hours of work per month for that level of extra income. Maybe that's enough to get you out of debt, or cover your car payment, school tuition, or little league fees. Read Chapter 10 to see what $100 monthly can do for you if you invest it faithfully.

4. Ebay

Anyone—and I mean anyone—can make money on Ebay. What is Ebay? Magic! On www.ebay.com you can sell or buy almost anything. You can use it like a garage sale to sell things that you already own and don't need anymore, or you can create a business in which you buy from manufacturers and resell those items in an online store. You can start with no money and sell your good used items online for cash. This incredible engine exposes you to hundreds of thousands of buyers all over the world. I have sold items as low-cost as $5.^{00} and as expensive as $1,500.^{00} on Ebay.

There are some rules to follow and methods to optimize your success on Ebay that are outside the scope of this book, so be sure to educate yourself before launching into an Ebay business. I recommend this book: *The Official Ebay Bible* by Jim Griffith (Gotham Books/Penguin Group). He tells you everything you would need to know to sell successfully on Ebay. I did what he said to do, step by step, and it worked perfectly. You'll need an online banking account called PayPal (www.paypal.com) for transferring money. It's easy to set up, and I recommend using PayPal's security token to protect your identity and money.

5. Arts and crafts

Arts and crafts festivals and arts and crafts stores are popular in some towns and cities. If you can make quality products and have a unique product or style, you may be able to supplement your income by selling homemade products. In certain months, depending where you live, there are shows almost every weekend. Find out about shows in your community, and attend a few of them. Ask questions of the people you meet there. Most of them are very friendly, and many of them know each other because they participate in several shows each year. Ask how they got started, how much the booths cost, how to get on a mailing list to find out about upcoming shows, how to be invited to future shows, and so forth. You may even be able to co-op and sell your projects on consignment in an established store or booth. Since we've already talked about Ebay, you're also thinking, *Couldn't I sell my own products on Ebay?* Yep.

6. Mail order

Mail-order businesses are relatively inexpensive to start and offer the advantage of working your business on your own time schedule. Post office boxes can be rented for about $30 per six-month contract. They provide privacy for you, and stability to your customer base. Even if you relocate to a new home, customers can still send correspondence to the same P.O. box number. Storefronts like UPS and Mail Boxes Etc. also offer delivery boxes, with the advantage that they can accept shipments from carriers like UPS and Fedex. A U.S. Postal Service P.O. box cannot accept shipments from those carriers. You can find prospective customers by

- advertising in local or national publications,

- buying mailing lists, which can be purchased from online services like www.directmail.com and www.usadata.com

- advertising online through powerful sites like Ebay and Craigslist, which expose thousands of prospective customers to your product.

Mail-order products can be homemade, bought from a manufacturer, or bought from a wholesaler. Wholesale prices are below retail, but usually you must buy in quantity to get those prices.

7. Writing for fun and profit

Do you write well? There are many possible formats and target markets for your writing. Do you like to travel? Do you take photos of interesting places while you're there? Consider submitting a freelance piece to travel or airline magazines. Are you skilled and experienced in a specialty like carpentry, electrical work, or gardening? You could submit a freelance piece to magazines that market to homeowners.

Could you write your own book? Maybe. Publishers need authors. You can submit your manuscript to publishers directly for consideration (be ready for many rejections; they have a lot of material to read). The most complete resource of contact information for the whole world of publishing is Robert Brewer's book *Writer's Market* (F+W media Inc./Writer's Digest Books) which is updated and published every year.

You may also consider self-publishing. There are three basic ways to do that:

- Use a local copier service such as Kinko's for an 8-1/2 by 11-inch format. This is not ideal and will cost more to print each book, but it's fast and easy.

- Work with a publisher that provides full editing, artwork, and short-run production services to authors, such as Essence Publishing (www.essencepublishing.com). This is a step lower in cost to print each book, but you'll have to print in quantities of at least 500 or 1,000.

- Create your own publishing company and work through an online print-on-demand partner like Lightning Source (www.lightningsource.com). This could be the lowest cost per book, and you won't have to purchase a large quantity. This option does, however, require more work and some technical expertise from you.

8. Child care

Child-care rates are high enough to make babysitting a worthwhile enterprise for many stay-at-home moms or dads. The average cost for day care is now about $70 to $100 a week for each child, so watching four or five children can make a big difference in your income. My friends who have built this type of business started out small, but their clientele grew quickly through word of mouth.

You will need to prepare your home according to criteria set by local and state laws, and obtain an inspection and license from your state. Four clients at $100 a week generates $1,600 to $2,000 monthly—a solid second income for your family. And this income enables one partner to stay at home with your own children while earning an income. Make sure to run this as a schedule C business or an LLC to minimize taxes on this income.

9. Your existing skills or hobbies

Whatever skill you have, for which your current employer pays you (or a former employer paid you), or for which you have been trained and/or licensed may be used in a business owned by you. Could you make an extra $100 a week doing handyman work? Painting houses? Repairing cars? Installing stereo equipment in homes or cars? Pinstriping or detailing cars? Mowing lawns? Cleaning pools? Playing music at a coffee house? Designing Web sites? Writing advertising copy? Balancing checkbooks? Doing accounting for a business on QuickBooks? Buying someone's groceries? (yes, there are professional shoppers who do this for the affluent or too-busy). Preparing and freezing packaged gourmet meals for them? Altering clothing? One of my friends who loves to cook, went to culinary school and started a Personal Chef business.

Whatever you do, set it up formally as a Schedule C or better yet, as an LLC to take advantage of tax laws and liability protection designed for businesses. Run it as a business, with separate bank accounts and good record-keeping. Then use 100 percent of the income for paying off your debt and building your savings and investments.

10. Basic rules for business

Whatever business you choose to build, these three factors will help it to grow and stabilize:

- Be a person of integrity. Work toward having an excellent reputation as a person and as a company, and your repeat customers and internal satisfaction will be the rewards.

- Be proud of what you make, create, write, or sell. Endeavor to be the best if you are providing a service; work toward perfect quality if you are manufacturing a product.

- Plan and schedule the time you will invest in your business, and keep your time commitments to your business as you would for your employer. Your future wealth or poverty depends on it.

NOTES

_____

_____

_____

_____

_____

_____

_____

_____

_____

_____

_____

_____

_____

_____

Chapter 7

AROUND THE HOUSE

"Dishonest money dwindles away,
but he who gathers money little by little makes it grow."
—Proverbs 13:11

This chapter is part of your Lifestyle Equalization, but this one focuses on your home. Remember to put your savings into an interest-bearing investment, or use it to erase debt!

1. Switch off

Keep unnecessary lights and appliances in your home turned off. Consider this: four 60-watt light bulbs running for sixteen hours use 3.8 kilowatt-hours. At ten cents per kilowatt-hour, running these four lights sixteen hours a day will cost you about $140 a year. This could be four separate lamps in your home, but the same calculation applies to many small chandelier-type fixtures holding six 40-watt bulbs or four 60-watt bulbs. This one fixture (usually one single wall switch), if left on sixteen hours a day, will cost you the same $140 a year.

The best way to conserve is to use natural light during the day and to use lights only in the room you are using during the evening, keeping lights in other rooms turned off. You may also consider compact fluorescent light (CFL) bulbs, which use much less energy than an incandescent bulb for a similar amount of light. They are more expensive to buy but can pay you back in the long run due to their more efficient energy usage. Buy them when they are on sale! Note: CFLs contain mercury, the second most toxic substance in the universe. Read the directions! Handle them carefully to prevent breakage, and then recycle them when they stop working. You can't just throw these bulbs into the trash.

2. Appliances

Appliances can use much more energy than your lights, so it is important to control your use of these too. The wattage rating is usually marked outside the appliance, or on a plate inside the unit, or in the literature provided by the manufacturer. Some typical numbers for electric appliances are shown in this table.

Central air conditioner	4,500 Watts
Clothes dryer	5,600 Watts
Conventional oven	4,400 Watts
Dishwasher	3,600 Watts
Hair dryer	1,500 Watts
Lawn blower/vacuum	935 Watts
Microwave oven	950 Watts
Personal computer	400 Watts
Pool pump	2,000 Watts
Range burner	900 Watts
Refrigerator	700 Watts
TV	200 Watts
VCR or DVD player	35 Watts
Video game	190 Watts
Washing machine	900 Watts
Water heater	5,000 Watts

Here is the calculation to use in determining your yearly cost:

(watts)/1000 × (hours per day) × (cost per kilowatt-hour) × (365 days)

You can see that using a microwave oven instead of a conventional oven saves about 75 percent of the electricity used to cook your food—even more, actually, because of the warm-up time of the oven. In the summertime, your air conditioner has to remove all that excess oven heat. Therefore using an oven has an extended effect on power consumption. In the winter, your conventional oven helps heat the home, offsetting some of your heating costs.

Some power companies charge for your peak demand as well as for your total kilowatt-hours used during the month. In this case, you can reduce your costs in the long run by installing a residential load-controller on your home. Such a device can pay for itself within a couple of years, because it constantly monitors and controls the peak demand by cycling high-usage appliances off and on. For example, it may turn off your water heater while the air conditioner is running, or turn on your pool pump only when both the water heater and air conditioner are not running.

There are several other less expensive products that can help control your energy costs. These will help whether your power company charges a demand rate or not. Most should be installed only by a qualified electrician.

- Automation systems are available from www.X10.com and www.smarthome.com for controlling lights and appliances in your home. The control unit connects to your home computer and can be programmed for a multitude of on/off times. Each lamp, light fixture or appliance can be individually scheduled to turn on or off independent of the rest of the lights and appliances in your house. I use it to control outdoor Christmas lights, and to command closet lights and outdoor lights to turn off several times a day, just in case we accidentally left them on.

- Water heater timer. These inexpensive timers will turn on your electric water heater at specific times throughout the day or night, and keep it off when you don't need it. For example, you can set it to turn the water heater on at 5 a.m. so that you will have hot water when you wake up. And then the timer can turn the water heater off again at 8 a.m. because you will be at work all day. If you can switch off just two hours of water heater use every day, it will save 5Kw × 2 hours × 365 days × 10 cents = $365 a year!

- Setback (programmable) thermostat. This device controls energy use like the water heater timer, by time of day. It sets your air conditioner (or heat pump) thermostat to a comfortable level automatically just before you come home and changes it to a less expensive level while you are gone each day. For example, in summer you can program it to let the house reach 90 degrees while you are at work during the day and automatically cool down to 77 degrees an hour before you come home. If you can avoid just two hours of run time daily, you'll save more than $300 a year.

- If you use outdoor lighting at night, make sure to use a light-sensor or timer to control it. That way the lights will use electricity only when necessary—not too early because you had to leave the house for the evening, and not too late because you slept in or forgot to turn off the lights before leaving the house.

- Individual timers and motion detectors are also available for the control of indoor lighting, which can help keep lights off when not in use. These can range from $5.^{00} for a simple timer that plugs into an AC outlet, to $30.^{00} for a wall-mounted unit that replaces your wall switch. Remember No. 1 at the beginning of this chapter: every four 60-watt bulbs that you turn off for an hour a day save about $10.^{00} a year. Switch off three or four light fixtures an extra four hours a day, and you've saved over $150 a year.

3. Proud and poor or humble and rich

If you are currently paying for pool service, lawn mowing, housekeeping, washing your car, or laundry service, consider this: would you rather be proud and poor, or humble and rich? Pride is a problem. It can keep us in financial bondage to that image. How much money would you save if you cleaned your own pool, mowed your own lawn, cleaned your own house, washed your own car, and laundered and pressed your own clothes? Yes, it will take more of your time. But if that's TV time or other wasted time, consider these numbers:

Pool service	$10.^{00} per week
Lawn service	$20.^{00} per week
Housekeeping	$20.^{00} per week
Car wash	$10.^{00} per week
Laundry/Pressing	$10.^{00} per week
TOTAL	$70.^{00} per week

That $70.^{00} per week adds up to $280 or more every month. And that $280 every month is $3,360 a year! Invested at 5 percent for 20 years, it will be $115,000. Let that sink in for a moment. Most of us don't worry about paying $20.^{00} for this service or $20.^{00} for that service. But those regular, ongoing payments can mean the difference between paying cash for a new sports car when you retire or driving the same car you're driving now, when it's 20 years older.

It can make the difference between traveling the world and volunteering your time to help others, or working behind the counter at the local fast-food restaurant when you're 70 years old.

What if you only use one of these services? It's still $20.^{00} a week, which is $1,040 a year or $32,000 in 20 years.

From now on, remember that ten dollars is not ten dollars. $10.^{00} twice a week is $1,000 a year! Anything that you used to throw $10.^{00} at regularly is costing you $1,000 a year. Would you take $1,000 out of your purse, wallet, or bank account and hand it over right now to your yard guy, your laundry service—to *anyone*?

You are already handing it over—$10.^{00} at a time.

4. Telephone solicitors

Never buy from telephone solicitors (at best they fall into the category of impulse buying; worst case they are stealing your identity and credit card number). Never, *ever* give your credit card number to anyone who calls your phone. You can eliminate most of these calls by registering your phone number with the national do-not-call list at www.donotcall.gov. This makes it illegal for telephone solicitors to call you; and it only takes about a month to become active after you register.

5. Newspaper subscription

If you subscribe to the local daily newspaper now and seldom read it or do not clip coupons, consider canceling the subscription and buying only the issues you want at a newspaper stand or convenience store. Or, if you travel often, many airlines and business hotels offer complimentary copies free every morning. It sounds petty, but $20.^{00} for eight weeks is $130 a year. If you have time to read only one issue per week at 50 cents each, you will spend only $26.^{00} per year for a savings of $104 a year. Most of the information in a newspaper is negative anyway, because bad news sells. Your attitude and speed to success will be better if you read positive books rather than a negative newspaper! If you are not using the coupons in the newspaper to save money, you could cancel your subscription—and its expense—altogether.

6. Leverage

It is worth mentioning again that owning a home is far better for your long-term financial growth than renting. Your home, in most areas of the country, will appreciate over time; on average, real estate always has. At the time of this writing, several areas of the country, including my own hometown, have endured a severe correction in market values (read: the value of my home dropped by half). This is in response to over-appreciation that drove prices too high during the previous few years. But the correction will be temporary, and real estate in these areas will appreciate again in the future. In fact, when the market is in a low correction like this, it is the *very best* time to buy.

The most important feature of real estate is *leverage*. Financial leverage is just like mechanical leverage. A small person can move a large, heavy object by applying a small force on the end of a lever (remember science class?). In the same way, financial leverage enables you to control a large asset with a relatively small amount of money. Let's compare investing without leverage, to investing *with* leverage.

Investing without leverage is a savings account or CD. When you deposit $100, you control $100, and your interest income is paid on $100. If you deposit $10,000, you control $10,000, and your interest income is based on $10,000. These are some of the safest but worst-performing investments because they have no leverage and pay low rates. But they are useful as a tool to capture funds and build your discipline. Once you have enough in the account, you can move a *portion* of those funds to leveraged investments.

Investing with leverage means depositing that same $10,000 as a down payment in a leveraged investment such as a house. It enables you to control $100,000 to $200,000 worth of assets— such as your own home or a rental property. A $10,000 deposit is 5 percent down payment on a $200,000 house, and the house may appreciate at 5 percent per year on average.

In 30 years, a savings account with a single $10,000 deposit, paying 5 percent a year, will be worth about $40,000. But a $200,000 house appreciating at 5 percent a year, will be worth over $800,000, Same $10,000 investment, 20 times the difference in net worth. *Leverage.*

7. Mortgage rate

Watch the mortgage interest rates carefully. If you previously bought or refinanced your home at 2 or 3 percentage points above the going rate, you can save yourself big monthly dollars by refinancing at the lower rate. It will also save a huge amount of the total finance charge over the life of the loan. There must be a substantial spread, however, between the old rate and the new rate, for this refinance to be worthwhile. This is because there are costs associated with refinancing, and you will want to recover those costs within a few months. Example: Suppose you owe $100,000 on your home, and it is financed for 30 years at a fixed rate of 8 percent. By refinancing at 6 percent, you will reduce your payment by more than $100 per month—$1,200 per year back into your investments or debt reduction plan. So if your refi costs are less than $1,200 and you're planning to stay in the home for more a few years, it's a great deal.

8. Optimize the cost of technology.

Switching from an expensive digital cable subscription with all the movie tiers to basic cable—even analog cable if it is available—can save $30.⁰⁰ to $40.⁰⁰ per month or $360 to $480 per year. That TV isn't making you any money anyway; you need to spend less time in front of it.

Using your cell phone or VOIP can mean free long distance to talk to your family and friends, rather than tens or hundreds of dollars a month using a land line. VOIP is Voice Over Internet Protocol (using your computer as a phone) and can range from a free service like Skype (www.Skype.com) to paid services for about $20.⁰⁰ to $30.⁰⁰ a month. You'll need a cheap headset or a phone with built-in VOIP capability, but these services work well and for a fraction of the cost of regular long-distance service on your land line.

You can even reduce the cost of your cell phone contract by right-sizing your plan for the number of minutes and text messages that you usually use. If you are paying $20.⁰⁰ a month for unlimited text, for example, but you use only 100 text messages each month, your carrier may have a plan for $5.⁰⁰ or $10.⁰⁰ a month that would cover your usage. Saving $10.⁰⁰ every month means putting $120 a year into your pocket or paying down a credit card.

Internet service is no longer a luxury; it is a necessity for today's communication, jobs and schoolwork. But your internet service provider may offer different connection speeds at different prices. We changed ours from the very fastest to the next-to-slowest, saving about $20.^{00} every month ($240 a year), and honestly we can't tell the difference in the speed.

9. Eliminate storage fees.

If you are paying for storage of your belongings, consider when you last used them, needed them, or even saw them! Many of us pay monthly storage fees for old stuff that we'll never use again. Consider selling some of it on Ebay, throwing some of it away, giving some of it to charity (tax deduction!) and consolidating the rest into your living space. If your storage unit is costing you even $50.^{00} a month, that's $600 every year that could go toward paying off a credit card. Or invest that amount at 5 percent, and it will be more than $7,500 in ten years. Even if you have to build a $500 shed in your back yard to store everything, you'll recover that cost in a year and save $50.^{00} every month—$600 every single year—from then on.

10. Coupon crash course

A word about your home grocery bill: coupons! Proper use of coupon-clipping can save you a *lot* of money. My wife became an Olympic-level coupon-clipper during a time when we were facing bankruptcy and pinching pennies, and it saved us. How? *Strategy*. We literally got toothpaste, shampoo, and toilet paper for *free*. The key is to organize your coupons in a notebook so that you can keep track of them, and never use a coupon until the item goes on sale.

Then use both the sale and the coupon together for ridiculous savings.

There is one reason to have a Sunday newspaper delivered to your door each week: clip and use the coupons. You can also download and print coupons from Web sites like these:

www.couponmom.com
www.coupons.com
www.couponsense.com

What if the coupon is for a brand you don't like? We decided to change our taste, and now we like the brands that are one half to one tenth the price of other brands. Yes, I said *one tenth* the price. By changing your thinking, you can appreciate that off-brands–or any brand that happens to be on sale with a coupon–can help you get out of debt and build wealth for your family. Then your goals can become reality.

This technique can extend into other areas like gift wrapping paper. Buy it when it's on sale no matter what time of year, and you'll save money over the price you'll pay to wrap a last-minute gift. Buying solid colors enables you to use the same paper for very different occasions. What color do we like? The one that's on sale!

NOTES

Chapter 8

THE ART OF SELF-DISCIPLINE

"One man pretends to be rich, yet has nothing;
another pretends to be poor, yet has great wealth."
—Proverbs 13:7

One of the wealthiest people I personally know drives an older Ford pickup truck. Not a Mercedes or BMW, not a Lexus or a Ferrari. Not even a new pickup—a used one. He could have paid cash for any car he wanted, but he chooses to drive this pickup. Therefore, his money keeps working for him, generating more money in interest. Humble and rich, rather than proud and poor.

1. Practice...and practice.

Self-discipline was mentioned in an earlier chapter about budgeting. Here are some more ways to discipline yourself. After all, self-discipline is a learned art, not a natural ability from birth. The first rule to remember is practice, practice, practice. Just as practice can improve playing a sport or musical instrument or learning a new language, the more you practice anything, the better you will become. The converse is also true: without practice, you will never learn to discipline yourself, and the result will be less money in your wallet, purse, and bank accounts.

- Drive the speed limit. One ticket at $150 can erase your success in other areas, like the solid month you went without Starbucks so that you could double the payment on your credit card.

- Don't consolidate debt unless you are using the technique described in chapter 1 to move high-interest debt onto a low-interest vehicle; it is too easy to ring those other cards right back up. Discipline means attacking each debt one at a time until all of your debts are gone. The only exception is transferring high-interest debt to a lower-interest vehicle, such as moving debt from a 26 percent credit card to an 8 percent credit card. If you do this, destroy the high-interest card so that you won't be tempted to charge it back up.

- Don't carry extra credit cards in your purse or wallet. Only spend what you decide beforehand, in cash. You might want to keep one card with you for emergencies or car rental and hotel while traveling, but you'll only need one card for that.

- If you're not bringing your lunch to work, then use this discipline: you will only eat out if you have a coupon for a discount!

- Check and track your bills weekly to make sure you pay them on time. One $30.^{00} late fee per month is $360 a year. You may even use an online service like www.mycheckfree.com to pay some of your bills. It lets you program the bills ahead of time to be automatically paid from your checking account on the day they are due, or a day or two early, so that you don't have to worry about mail arriving late.

- If you discover during your weekly bill review that you've waited too long and a bill will be late by the time you mail it, go online to the provider's Web site. Your insurance company, city water company, gas, electric, phone and others probably have a way for you to pay the bill online, saving a stamp ($.42 × 12 = $6.^{00} = lunch) and avoiding a costly late fee. If you can pay 20 bills online every month, you'll save $.42 × 20 × 12 months = $100 a year in postage!

- Use your toothpaste, shampoo, conditioner, and other products *until they are really empty.* Shake the bottles down & leave them upside down to get every drop; then add water and shake them up to get an extra week after that.

Squeeze the toothpaste tube from every angle until it truly has no more to give. If you can get two more weeks out of any of them, that's two more weeks you got to use your money before giving it up. Money in your pocket at the end of the year. Maybe it will help you to pay something on time and avoid a late fee, or pay early to reduce finance charges.

- Pay financed bills (car, credit cards, mortgage) early if you can. This reduces the finance charge, putting more of your payment toward the principal (amount you owe) and less toward the finance charge. Bankrate has a variety of (free!) calculators at www.bankrate.com/calculators.aspx that are quick and easy to use.

2. Time management

You *must* become disciplined in managing your time so that you can

- make progress in starting and running your business

- be effective and efficient in your job

- ensure that you have family time and personal time

- exercise and rest

- do all of it without going crazy.

More than managing time, you have to take hold of it and force it to do your will. The simplest way to start is to buy and use an inexpensive daily planner. These are available in most department and office-supply stores for as little as $20.^{00}. Be sure to choose one that is small enough to carry with you all the time. Start with one that shows you the entire week on one page, with a section for each day. Each daily section should have time slots in one-hour or half-hour increments.

At the beginning of each week, dedicate thirty minutes to plan and organize your time for that week in blocks of thirty minutes to one hour. Start with the activities that you know you will have to do. Make sure to reserve time for your budget, your family, yourself, exercise, spiritual growth, and your business ventures.

Likewise, at the end of each day, plan the next day. You could also do this in the morning before starting your day; it really doesn't matter when, as long as you do it regularly. Personally, I sleep better if I unload the list from my mind to a piece of paper before going to bed. The important thing is to do your planning at the same time every day and every week. That way it will become a habit, and you will have reached your first goal in self-discipline!

3. Time systems

After mastering No. 2 and successfully using a basic planner for a few months, you may want to move up to a more complete time and activity organizer from Day-Timer® at www.daytimer.com, FranklinCovey® at www.franklincovey.com or Day Runner® at www.dayrunner.com. All of these companies offer *systems* built around the basic planner described in No. 2. Franklin is the most advanced and even provides an audio time-management tool that teaches you how to manage your life by using their system. The binders typically have monthly calendars, daily planners, a phone directory, filing sections, and pockets and tabs for organizing information.

It's like carrying a portable office with you—all your important information is at your fingertips. The binders come in various sizes, from pocket-size to 5 by 7 inches to 8-1/2 by 11 inches. You can also customize the contents to fit your needs and preferences. These are great for self-discipline, because once you start using a system like this for a month, you will wonder how you ever survived without it. You'll never give it up.

4. PDA

You may decide to use an electronic version such as a PDA (Personal Digital Assistant). These are available from several different manufacturers. At this writing, many cellular telephones provide this function as well, especially "smart phones" such as the Palm® Treo™, RIM Blackberry®, Samsung Blackjack™ and Apple® iPhone™. These portable devices usually provide a software desktop version that runs on your PC or laptop computer, which is easier for typing lots of data and is an effective backup. Or they communicate with your existing time management software such as Microsoft Outlook. The advantages of these products are as follows:

- they hold a huge amount of information in a very small package

- they are usually with you, so you will use them,

- they can beep to remind you of an important task or meeting!

A very important, universal rule for electronic systems: _Electronic data does not exist until it is stored in at least two places._ This is because a portable device can be lost or stolen; or it can fail electronically at the worst possible time. Ask anyone who has forgotten to backup (save the data from their portable device) to a PC for several weeks and then has broken or lost his or her handheld device. The loss of data can cause much heartburn, and a lot of lost time! Better to connect the PDA to your PC at least once a week to save the information. If the PC is a laptop and it is usually with you and your PDA, well, back to Rule No. 1. Back up the laptop onto a thumb drive, external hard disk, or writeable CD or DVD, and keep that backup copy in a safe, separate location from the PDA and laptop.

Use passwords to protect your privacy and information, otherwise the loss of a PDA or laptop can have even worse consequences. Imagine your account numbers, bank passwords, or other personal data falling into the wrong hands.

5. Creating habits

Enough about organization tools; how do we get there? How do we become disciplined enough to use our own system, whether it is a paper system or an electronic one? Here is an extremely powerful rule of thumb: A human being takes about twenty-one days to create a habit (or to break one). Think about that for a moment. If you can force yourself to do something—anything—for twenty-one days straight, your subconscious mind will accept it as normal routine, and you will have formed a habit. You can use this to break undesirable habits or to make new, positive ones.

Think about some of the ideas in the first few chapters. Could you try one or two of these, every day for twenty-one days? If you do this (and you absolutely can), you will be surprised next month how easy it has become to put money in the bank or to reduce your debt. When you measure your progress in three months, you will be even more amazed. Cash will be in the bank (or your debt load will be smaller), and you will be ready to take on the next step in your financial master plan. The first and simplest techniques will have become routine for you.

6. Schedule meetings with yourself.

Set aside a specific time each day and each week to think, work on your business ideas, pay bills, update your budget, review your goals, and plan your time. Put it into your planning system as a firm appointment that you will not break. By scheduling repetitive activities at the same time every day or the same day every week, you will more quickly assimilate them into habits. Once they become automatic, you are ready to add another money-saving or money-growing technique to your tool kit.

7. Setting goals

Set specific goals. Without specific goals, human beings are less motivated; we have no way to measure our progress and therefore less incentive to strive for improvement. But specific, well-defined goals challenge us to find solutions and energize us to work toward those solutions. This applies to financial goals for sure. But just as important, it applies to personal growth, professional growth, spiritual growth, any area of self-discipline or self-improvement.

8. Write it down.

Write your goals down. This is critical to your success. Keep a copy of them with you, all the time. Post them where you can see them every day. When you have a little spare time while waiting for the bus or sitting in your doctor's office or the airport, take them out and read them again. Write them down again, every day or every week. Look at your goals every morning when you wake up and every night before you go to sleep. Your subconscious mind does not know the difference between an idea and reality. The more you focus and review your goals, the more your subconscious mind will accept them as fact, furnish you with ideas, help you to change your actions, and move you toward those goals.

9. Talk to yourself.

Practice talking to yourself. Reinforce your goals and your ability to achieve them by reciting them out loud every day. Say them in the present tense. Rather than "I hope to have one thousand dollars saved by this time next year," say out loud, "I am so happy now that I have made an extra thousand dollars." Most successful people got that way by keeping their goals at the forefront of their mind and by believing they could achieve those goals. Think about your goals every morning when you wake up. Say them out loud to program your subconscious mind. Make it a habit to do this, and then work your plan for that day.

Avoid saying anything negative, even in jest. Remember that your subconscious mind does not know the difference between good programming and bad programming, or between an idea and reality. Your mind is a computer that will work on whatever you feed it. You do not need to remind yourself of past failures or future fears; somebody else will do that for you! Only program your mind with positive information, confirmation that you will reach your goals, that you _can_ do it. Indeed, that you have already done it.

10. Break it down.

Break your goals down into manageable chunks. Start with a five-year goal, and break it down into goals for each year. Then move a step farther, and decide what you must do in each of the next twelve months to reach the first year goal. Then break each monthly goal into weekly objectives, which you can reasonably manage. Those weekly objectives drive the priorities that you'll enter into your daily planning system or calendar.

You can change any of the goals or milestones anytime, if you want to. The important thing is to get everything on paper, right now, and then transform it into manageable pieces in your daily planner. Then you will be well on your way!

My five-year goals:

_____

_____

_____

_____

_____

My goals for this year:

_____

_____

_____

_____

Steps each month to reach those goals:

1. _____

2. _____

3. _____

4. _____

5. _____

6. _____

7. _____

8. _____

9. _____

10. _____

11. _____

12. _____

NOTES

Chapter 9

GET SMART

"Blessed is the man who finds wisdom,
the man who gains understanding,
for she is more profitable than silver
and yields better returns than gold.
She is more precious than rubies;
nothing you desire can compare with her.
Long life are in her right hand;
in her left hand are riches and honor."
—Proverbs 3:13-16

1. Education and action

The first step in "Get Smart" is to educate yourself in specific information that will move you toward your goals. Then *do* what you have learned. "Smart" has nothing to do with your IQ or formal education level. It means learning all you can and using what you learn to achieve your goals. You were already smart to buy this book; you will be smarter after you read it and even smarter when you *do* what you have learned.

Reading is the first recommendation here. Find the books in any good bookstore, or discounted online at www.amazon.com, www.alibris.com, or www.discountbooksale.com, or in the library for free. Some of these can be downloaded as e-books or purchased online for a dollar or two and will return many thousands back to you, if you use their wisdom. Choose your reading list carefully; it is important to be efficient and to maximize the return on your time investment. Some recommendations are given below. You might start with this one. It's been around since 1926, it's a short and easy read, and it will tell you the bottom-line secrets for saving and growing your money:

- *The Richest Man in Babylon* by George S. Clason (Penguin books, Signet Books).

There is another book that's been around longer; you may have noticed that it's the source of my quotes at the beginning of each chapter: the Holy Bible. It has a lot to say about the source of money, the purpose of money, and how to handle money. And just about everything else in your life—a great instruction manual. There are a number of good translations but I recommend a modern one (translated in the twentieth century or later) such as New International Version or New American Standard Version or paraphrased in The Living Bible. The Amplified Bible is also useful, as it helps expand some of the ancient languages into modern English, where a word-for-word translation may lack some of the richness and depth of the original text.

2. Immigrants and other self-made millionaires

Most millionaires in this country did not inherit their money; they built their own wealth. Many started with nothing. Here are two books that teach the creation of wealth by lifestyle equalization and building something from nothing:

- *Self-Made in America* by John McCormack (Perseus Books)

- *The Millionaire Next Door* by Thomas J. Stanley and William D. Danko (Pocket Books/Simon & Schuster).

These books will radically change your thinking about what is possible for anyone—and I mean *anyone*. If you are reading *100 Ways to Save and Grow Your Money* in English, you are already ahead of some of the people described in these books. They came to this country with zero money and no ability to read or speak English; yet they became millionaires. Opportunity is limited only by our thinking. Therefore, ...

3. Expand your thinking.

Broaden and raise the bar in your thinking—one of the most important things you can do to improve your life and potential for success. Here are two books that will help you do that:

- *The Magic of Thinking Big* by Dr. David A. Schwartz (Fireside Books)
- *The Power of Positive Thinking* by Norman Vincent Peale (Fawcett Crest or Running Press Books or Simon & Schuster Audio)

These two books will open your thinking to the reality that you *can* accomplish what you set out to do. Another classic that still holds true today is:

- *Think and Grow Rich* by Napoleon Hill (Fawcett Books)

Hill interviewed five hundred wealthy men of his time and distilled their wisdom into this book—a step-by-step process for changing your thinking, achieving your goals, increasing your wealth, and upgrading your ability to help others.

4. Be different.

Rhinoceros Success by Scott Alexander (The Rhino's Press, Inc.) is a great motivational book designed to wake us up to a funny fact. It's not only OK to be different; it is actually *required*, in order to be successful! If we continue to do what everyone else does, we will end up in the same financial condition: broke and in debt. By focusing on our goal of financial freedom for our family and working our plan—acting differently from the norm in our society—we will have something wonderfully different: freedom, peace, and the ability to help others.

5. Listen and learn.

Books are not the only way to get smart. Audiocassettes, compact discs, audio downloads and podcasts (digital mp3 audio files) are available from a variety of sources and can be used to make your driving, flying, or commute time more productive. Audio series are available for a wide range of topics, including foreign languages, customer-oriented selling, prayer, books of the Bible, goal-setting, organization, and motivation. There are even audio versions of some of the books recommended here. Listening to an audio version beats trying to calculate the time it will take you to crawl to the next intersection in rush-hour traffic.

I recommend books and audio by these excellent and successful teachers: Brian Tracy at www.briantracy.com, Steve Chandler at www.stevechandler.com, and Earl Nightingale www.nightingale.com. Once you buy the recordings, you can transfer them to your MP3 player and carry a pretty large audio library in your pocket. Get a used MP3 player for low cost on Ebay!

6. Shoring up your marriage and relationships

Saving and growing your money will be smoother if your relationships are also running smoothly. One of the most common sources of friction in marriage—and a major factor in many divorces—is stress over family finances. Ask anyone who's actually been through a divorce, and they'll tell you that divorce is far more expensive than a good book and a good counselor. Here are some of the best books for improving communication and relationships:

- *Men are from Mars, Women are from Venus* by Dr John Gray (Harper Collins)

- *His Needs, Her Needs* by Willard F. Harley Jr. (Revell/Baker Book House)

- *The Love Dare* by Stephen Kendrick and Alex Kendrick (B&H Publishing Group)

- *Your Time-Starved Marriage* by Drs. Les and Leslie Parrott (Zondervan)

- *Love and Respect* by Dr. Emerson Eggerichs (Thomas Nelson)

You may choose to read these books together as a couple, or alone. Either way, they will increase the probability that your marriage will survive, stronger and happier.

7. One house × twenty years = financial Independence

This one must be done carefully in order to avoid losing what you have already gained: Learn how to safely purchase and manage one rental property. Not ten, not a hundred—just one. Do this only after you have paid off all your other debt and have a year's worth of living expenses in the bank. This is because the only constants in real estate are change and surprise. The surprises are usually not happy ones.

There are a number of books on the subject by a number of gurus. I love these guys, but most of them would like to sell you more books and seminars than you need. Unless you are going to change professions into full-time real estate investing, you don't need a $5,000 seminar or a $20,000 seminar. Read a couple of books on the subject to learn the basics and get your feet wet, such as *Millionaire Real Estate Mentor: the Secrets to Financial Freedom through Real Estate Investing* by Russ Whitney (Dearborn Trade Publishing, 2003). Then work with an experienced investor or property manager to help you get started.

[Note: If you do decide to dive into serious real estate investing as a career, the most complete system that I've found is Kris Kirschner's Autopilot® system. Autopilot is a *complete system* for buying and selling houses, everything you need to know in a 3-day or 5-day course with reams of reference material to take home. At this time, the course costs about 1/2 to 1/10 the cost of "boot camps" offered by others. And in my humble opinion, Autopilot teaches more complete, lower-risk methods. www.autopilotrealestate.com.]

The reason for owning one rental property is this: in fifteen to thirty years, the rent will have paid off the mortgage. Then you'll have a retirement income of $1,000 a month on top of Social Security and any other investment income. That's because after paying off the mortgage, the rent becomes pure income for *you*. Your $5,000 leveraged investment now can return more than twice that amount every few months at retirement.

One of my friends bought a condo for $60,000 with cash he had made in the stock market. He is in great shape already, because the tenant pays him more than $600 a month. There is no mortgage, so the monthly carrying cost is low. That means most of the rent is pure income for his family. If the tenant leaves and he has a vacancy for two months, it's no problem. That property will continue to generate income for the next thirty years, producing $600 × 12 × 30 = $216,000 in income. That doesn't count annual increases in rent, or interest he will earn on the rent if he reinvests the rent money. Because it is also appreciating, the property may be worth two to three times its current value, maybe $150,000, by the time my friend retires from his job. Adding that to the rent income totals more than $350,000 plus interest on the invested rent. Not a bad use of $60,000 in cash.

Another option would have been to use leverage: buying the property with a mortgage and only 10 percent down in cash. He'd still have $54,000 to invest elsewhere, and he'd still have the $150,000 appreciation over the next thirty years. The downside is that any vacancy chews up all the monthly profits in this case and can cause a real crisis if it lasts very long.

Don't want to keep managing a rental after retirement? OK, you can sell the property then. A $100,000 property today may be worth $200,000 to $300,000 when you retire. You can live on the cash or invest it and take the interest as income.

The basics are as follows:

- Create an LLC to hold the property. Don't hold it in your own name, because the winner in any lawsuit can take anything the owner owns. If you are personally the owner, that means *you* can personally lose everything. Using an LLC to buy and own the property can help to protect your personal assets from liability in case something goes horribly wrong.

- Buy the property with a low down payment or "subject-to" the existing financing (the loan stays in seller's name in that case, and you do not have to qualify for a new mortgage). Unless you have 2x to 3x the purchase price in cash reserves, don't pay cash for the house even if you could; that would cancel the leverage you can achieve by paying only 5 percent or 10 percent down. And paying cash without having 2x that cash in hand, would mean that you'd have no reserves for emergencies. Use the rest of your money for safe investments, holding back a liquid reserve fund to cover vacancies and unexpected repairs.

- Don't buy the property in a low-income area or slum. Buy it in a bread-and-butter, middle-class community. The cheapest properties may be that way for a reason: the windows are routinely broken, trash is routinely everywhere, the appliances are routinely stolen, and the rent collector's life might routinely be in danger. Play it safe, and buy in a reasonable area.

- Only buy a property whose known costs and potential costs—monthly payments, HOA fees, insurance, taxes, one month vacancy, 10 percent for management, and 10 percent for repairs—are still below the amount you can charge for rent. You will have to search carefully for this property, as they are in the minority. Don't buy the first house you find unless it meets all these criteria. If the mortgage is $700 a month and rent in that area is $900 a month, you might think the cash flow is $200 in the positive. But there are other monthly carrying costs to consider:

Mortgage payment	$700
HOA fees	$100
Maintenance & repairs	$50
10% vacancy	$90
Management	$90
Insurance	$20
Warranty	$40
Total Carrying Cost	**$1,090**

In this example, you might end up with a $200 *negative* cash flow. So make sure to check every fact and figure before signing any papers.

- Look for four sides brick if possible, as opposed to stucco or wood siding. It's harder to damage brick (tenants are not always kind to our property).

- Get a home inspection, including termite inspection, before you buy.

- Purchase a landlord insurance policy that will cover fire, loss of rents in case of damage, and liability. You should also consider buying a $1 million personal liability policy; these can be had for about $400 a year. If holding the property in an LLC, your LLC should also carry a liability policy.

- Before buying, check the rents and vacancy rates in that neighborhood to make sure you will be able to rent the property quickly for the amount you need. Check with a real estate agent, or www.rentometer.com or www.rentals.com.

- After buying, make sure the property is spotless before advertising it for rent—especially the kitchen and bathrooms. Turn on the power, clean or replace the carpet, apply fresh paint, and "stage" it with some low-cost materials:

  ✓ A few vases
  ✓ New dish towels
  ✓ Silk plants in the kitchen
  ✓ Baking soda in the refrigerator to remove odors
  ✓ New shower curtains, towels, and more silk plants in the bathrooms

This will help prospective tenants to see themselves living there, and you'll rent the property much faster.

- Locate and ask your local REIA (Real Estate Investors Association—find yours at www.reiclub.com) about a quality property manager that is hired and trusted by other investors. There are more bad ones than good ones, so be very selective here. It will mean the difference between one month of vacancy per year and six months or more of vacancy, which will cost you a fortune in mortgage payments. Trust me on this. I have been there and lost thousands of dollars due to poor property managers.

- Don't believe what *anyone* says even if that person is your best friend or your brother; check *all* the facts for yourself. Nobody is more interested in protecting you than *you*. Buying the right property is the smartest thing you can do because of the incredible leverage that real estate offers. It will pay you many times over for the rest of your life. But buying the wrong one can wipe out all the rest of your financial increase and create debt that takes years or decades to recover.

8. Read, filter, and do.

Read financial publications like *Kiplinger's* and *Money*—for free at the library. Much of the material is related to stock and bond investments, which may or may not be for you. But some issues give very practical methods for saving and growing your money, like installing low-flow shower heads, fixing leaky toilets, or getting the most vacation for your dollar. Filter this info down to what is safe and useful for you, and then do it.

9. Back to school

You can increase your education through university or community college courses. This could be learning another language to help you set up an import/export company or communicate with property buyers or tenants who do not speak English. Or education might increase your value to your employer to help that business become more profitable. Education might help you take the next upward steps in your career. It could be course work toward a real estate license, a business degree—whatever matches your immediate and long-term goals.

If the cost of tuition is a challenge, there are options available for help. You can apply for a student loan or a grant from the government. You can audit college courses for a much smaller fee than full tuition (but you cannot earn a degree this way). Correspondence and online courses are also available, some of which are fully accredited and allow you to work at your own pace. Your employer may even offer a tuition-reimbursement program that pays all or part of your tuition.

Dedicated three-month money management courses are also available from Crown Financial Ministries www.crown.org and Dave Ramsey's Financial Peace University www.daveramsey.com.

10. Other people's money

If your employer pays for tuition at three-day short courses and seminars, take advantage of the ones that make sense for your job and your goals. Courses in effective writing, customer-oriented selling, proposal and business plan writing, project management, presentation skills, marketing and so on can only help you in the long run. Every little bit that you add to your "smartness" better equips you to reach your goals and increases your value as an employee.

NOTES

Chapter 10

FUTURE SHOCK

*"Plans fail for lack of counsel,
but with many advisers they succeed."—Proverbs 15:22*

*"Commit to the LORD whatever you do,
and your plans will succeed."—Proverbs 16:3*

1. Start now.

Will you be able to survive on Social Security benefits alone when you retire? Will Social Security still be available when you retire? Many who draw Social Security benefits today, do not enjoy a lifestyle very far above poverty level. The federal poverty guideline this year for a single individual is $10,830 or $902 a month; $14,570 or $1214 a month for a couple. The maximum Social Security retirement benefit for a 66-year old is $2323 a month. Think carefully. It is not too early to start planning for your retirement, even if you are only 18 years old. The earlier you start, the less money you will have to put aside each month to reach your retirement income goal. And it is not too late to start, even if you are in your 50s. So, start putting *something* aside now.

The following table will give you some idea what you can achieve by saving regularly. The totals are calculated at thirty years with 7 percent interest, and forty-five years with 10 percent interest. There are many different investment vehicles to choose from, and each will provide a different level of risk and a different rate of return. This book is not intended to provide advice on which investments to choose.

Monthly Savings	Total after 30 years at 7%	Total after 45 years at 10%
$10	$12,199	$104,825
$50	$60,998	$524,125
$100	$121,997	$1,048,250
$500	$609,985	$5,241,250
$1,000	$1,219,970	$10,482,501

Did you realize that you can be a millionaire by the time you retire, with the use of discipline in your savings plan? Even a *multi-millionaire*? You can see that both the interest rate and the length of savings time have a big impact on the future total.

Take the time to find the best rates and build a foundation of safe investment vehicles. To get 10 percent annual return, your risk will be higher, but the rewards are evident in the table above. Ideally, you'll want to put most of your money in the safest (usually lower-yielding) investments, and a smaller percentage of your money in higher-risk, higher-yielding investments:

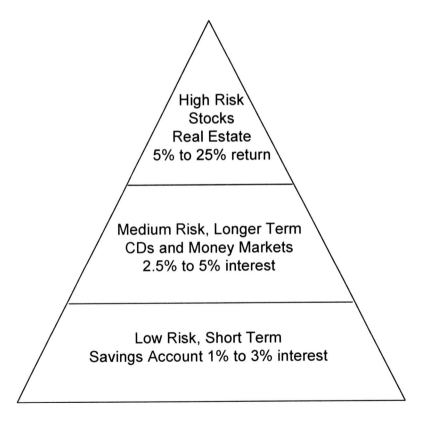

And you must remember that tax strategy is an important part of your savings plan, because the totals shown depend on compound interest. If the interest you earn is taxed every year, the totals will be smaller. One way to make sure your money will remain yours is to use an IRA or self-employed retirement savings plan, because the taxes are deferred. There are other tax-free vehicles such as overfunded insurance policies and Roth IRAs, which your financial planner can help to set up. Interest on U.S. savings bonds can also be tax-deferred if used for education.

2. College savings

Want to send your children to college, or just give them a healthy financial start after high school? Your disciplined monthly savings plan can add up to more than you might think. Let's look at two different interest rates, one which you might find in a passbook savings or CD account, and the other which you may find in a Roth education IRA, savings bond, money market or mutual fund:

Monthly Savings	Total after 18 years at 2%	Total after 18 years at 5%
$10	$2,597	$3,492
$50	$12,987	$17,460
$100	$25,974	$34,920
$500	$129,870	$174,601
$1,000	$259,740	$349,202

U.S. Savings bonds offer the advantage of tax-free interest if used for educational purposes (and tax-deferred interest otherwise). And in case you're having trouble with the discipline to buy them regularly, you can purchase these bonds through automatic payroll deduction.

3. Cash for cars

Rather than buying a new car on credit and paying a high rate of interest for 5 years, consider a radically different method. Buy a used car for $2,000 to get you around for those five years, while making monthly deposits to a savings account instead of monthly car payments. Then pay *cash* for a new car. In other words, make payments to *yourself.* That way you *earn* the interest instead of paying interest to the bank. As an example, let's consider a new car costing $20,000. At 9% interest, a 60-month loan payment would be about $415 per month. At that rate, you would pay the bank about $25,000 over the five-year life of the loan, and you'd have an old car to trade in at that point in time. Then you would start all over again with a new loan. In order to always own a fairly new car, you would be in debt for the rest of your life—and always paying 25 percent extra for the cost of the car.

Consider instead this method of paying *yourself* for five years:

At 5.5 percent interest rate (the rate you *earn* rather than pay), you can save $20,000 in five years by making a monthly payment (to yourself) of $291. That saves about $124 every month compared to making a car payment to the bank, more than $7,400 over the life of the saving program. That $7,400 can be used to pay off other debt, or build your retirement fund, or pay for college. Now when you purchase the car, you will own it free and clear. Another benefit is that anytime during the life of your "loan" to yourself, if an emergency arises, just borrow from yourself at 5.5 percent interest rather than from a bank at 15 percent. Think about it!

Using this method, you'll always drive a new car, and pay less for it than anyone who's making payments to the bank.

A book that describes this concept in detail, and how to use it to manage your money, is *Becoming Your Own Banker: The Infinite Banking Concept* by R. Nelson Nash (Infinite Banking Concepts).

4. Growing the family, growing the home

Planning for growth in your family? Maybe a room addition or new furniture, but ten years is so far away that you don't want to worry about it? This table will help you design and build a home repair, home addition, or furniture fund:

Monthly Savings	Total after 10 years at 2%	Total after 10 years at 5%
$10	$1,327	$1,553
$50	$6,636	$7,764
$100	$13,272	$15,528
$500	$66,360	$77,641
$1,000	$132,720	$155,282

5. Life insurance

Be wary of insurance plans advertised as a great investment (Whole Life or Universal Life). Their monthly premiums can be 10 times the monthly premium of Term Life plans. There are advanced investment strategies involving the overfunding of those policies that can provide tax-exempt growth, but your financial status has to be pretty bulletproof to do this safely. You should only consider those strategies after you have at least one year of income set aside, all debt is paid off, and you have at least $10,000 of excess cash to start plus another $1,000 a month to invest. If your financial picture is that strong, certified financial planners like Partners for Prosperity (www.partners4prosperity.com) can help with that kind of program.

For most people, it is enough to have a low-cost term life insurance policy to protect your family in the event of your death. A $250,000 term life policy might cost $25.^{00} a month compared to $250 a month, or more, for Whole Life or Universal Life. That's $300 a year compared to $3,000 a year! Better to buy the term policy and invest the difference in debt elimination and growth of your family's wealth.

6. Be a hundred-thousand-aire.

If you are a homeowner, consider a couple of ways to pay off your mortgage early. Why? Because on a thirty-year fixed mortgage, you will pay for your house about three times. *Three times!* For example, let's say the payments on your $150,000 home are $1,200 a month. $1,200 multiplied by 360 months (thirty years) is $432,000, and that's all out-of-pocket (out of your pocket and into the bank's pocket).

Many mortgage companies offer a fifteen-year, fixed-rate mortgage. The interest rate is usually a little lower than the interest on a thirty-year note, so the difference in payments may not be as much as you might expect. But you will save about $150,000 in payments on a $150,000 loan by paying it off in fifteen years instead of thirty years (these amounts are approximate—they depend on your interest rate and escrow impounds). On a $250,000 home it saves about $250,000. That's a quarter million dollars into your family's wealth.

7. Pay off a thirty-year mortgage early.

If you have a thirty-year, fixed-rate mortgage now, you can pay off your mortgage in 22 to 25 years without going through a refinance by making one extra payment per year. That's because the extra payment goes straight to the principal (balance owing) on your mortgage. Every payment after that extra payment, pays more principal than it would have, because the portion of the payment going to interest is reduced. This method can save you tens of thousands of dollars, maybe $100,000 or more, in payments and finance charges. It also saves a few thousand dollars in refinance costs that you didn't pay. You can try different extra-payment options with this great (free!) mortgage calculator at

www.bankrate.com/calculators/mortgages/mortgage-calculator.aspx

8. No prepayment penalty

Get an amortization schedule from your lenders for each debt that you owe. This schedule shows each month of the life of the loan and provides the amount of principal and interest associated with each payment. When you first take out the loan, most of the payment is going to interest (very little goes to reduction of the debt). Gradually, more and more of the payment is applied to the principal. At the end of the loan, almost all of the payment goes toward the principal. Make sure you have a simple interest loan with no penalty for prepayment. Then you can reduce both the length of your loan and the amount of the finance charge, by paying a little extra toward the principal with each monthly payment. Bankrate's calculators, already mentioned, can help you quickly determine the payoff time and dollar savings.

9. Ten dollars is a thousand dollars.

Remind yourself often about the time-value of money. That $10.^{00} burning a hole in your pocket right now may *seem* like only $10.^{00}, but invested into a tax-exempt, interest-bearing financial program (or even a simple passbook savings account), it will be worth much more in a few years. If you spend it now on a depreciating item (and most things that money can buy *will* depreciate the moment you take them out of the store), you are moving backward. Remember that $10.^{00} is not $10.^{00}. Ten dollars twice a week is more than $1,000.^{00} a year.

This is not to say that every dime you earn should be saved forever; on the contrary, our economy would collapse if nobody ever bought anything. But you must have a plan, and follow that plan, to reach your goals. That will involve some sacrifice and discipline. Every reader of this book has the ability to achieve financial freedom. Will you? Are you willing to pay the price for a few years to secure your future?

10. Make it happen.

Start now. Whatever you decide to do, no matter which of the *100 Ways* you want to use first, no matter how good or ugly your present situation is, *don't wait!* If you don't start doing something new and different as soon as you put this book down, the normal human response will be to forget all the material you've just learned. You'll lose sight of your motivation, accept your present status as it is, and stay in bondage. If you don't start immediately, a month from now you won't even remember reading the book.

Achievement of your goals will not happen by accident; the world will not lay a chunk of gold at your feet. You have to make it happen. And it *will* happen, if you start now and learn to discipline yourself. You do not have to earn $100,000 a year now to be a millionaire in 20 or 30 years. You just have to manage the money and income you *already have* effectively and work toward increased income. If you do earn more than $100,000 a year now, great! You can use the *100 Ways* to safeguard yourself against emergency, retire earlier, give to excellent charitable causes, and live a more satisfied life.

When you have setbacks (and you will), don't panic. Cover whatever emergency has arisen with money you have saved, and then get back on track as soon as possible. Have I done everything in this book perfectly? No! I have made more and larger financial mistakes than most people on the planet. (That is how most of this was learned—the hard way!). If I can do it, you can do it.

If you can simply, over time, change your habits to save $10.^{00} a month in each of seventeen categories, you can become a millionaire before you retire. Small steps, consistently, will have *big* results:

- Save $10.^{00} on monthly groceries by eating leftovers or reducing snacks.
- Save another $10.^{00} on monthly groceries by using coupons and loyalty card.
- Save $10.^{00} on monthly gasoline by carpooling or taking a shorter route.
- Save $10.^{00} on monthly eating out by ordering water instead of a soda.
- Save $10.^{00} on monthly entertainment by not ordering popcorn at the movies.
- Save $10.^{00} on monthly coffee by skipping just two or three days.
- Save $10.^{00} on monthly car insurance by shopping or changing the deductible.
- Change your W-4 to receive an extra $10 a month net.
- Save $10.^{00} on monthly electricity by turning off lights when not in the room.
- Gain $10.^{00} in monthly income from your job by asking for a raise.
- Save $10.^{00} a month by switching from an expensive gym to the YMCA.
- Save $10.^{00} a month by *not* buying impulse items at the checkout.
- Save $10.^{00} a month on your next car by buying pre-owned or one fewer option.
- Save $10.^{00} a month on taxes by donating used items instead of throwing them away.
- Earn $10.^{00} a month selling unnecessary items on Ebay.
- Save $10.^{00} a month in credit card interest by paying off a small one.
- Save $10.^{00} a month in The Jar.

Total: $170.^{00} a month or $2,000.^{00} every year.

What if you save $10.^{00} in each category, $2,000 a year for forty years, and earn 10 percent average during that time? Here is the model for a 25-year old, saving $10.00 on each of seventeen items consistently for forty years until retirement at age 65:

25-year old, $10 per month × 17 items	Traditional IRA	Roth IRA
Amount deposited with discipline	$2,000	$2,000
Interest rate	10%	10%
Value after 40 years	$1,054,013	$1,054,013
Tax on withdrawals at 25% tax rate	$263,503	$0
Net usable cash	**$790,510**	**$1,054,013**

You are a millionaire already, if you implement this plan today. After that, you're just waiting for your million to be deposited. How do you find a 10 percent return? Well, that will have to be the subject for another book. Self-directed accounts can be used to invest in real estate, mutual funds, stock and other investments, which can provide returns this high. Some real estate investors pay up to 13 percent to Private Lenders (someone like you). What if you can only find 5 percent return for your investment? This frugal 25-year old will still end up with $250,000 net usable cash.

What if you're 35 years old and don't have 40 years to put money away for retirement? Let's take our $170 monthly ($2,000 a year) and add an annual $1,000 tax return, which you faithfully add to your savings portfolio in a money market account at 5 percent. This is how it looks:

35-year old, $10 per month × 17 items plus $1K tax return in money market	Traditional IRA	Roth IRA
Amount deposited with discipline	$2,000	$2,000
Tax return into money market annually	$1,000	$1,000
Interest rate in IRA	10%	10%
Interest rate in money market	5%	5%
IRA value after 30 years	$376,748	$376,748
Money market value after 30 years	$69,355	$69,355
Tax on IRA withdrawals at 25% tax rate	$94,187	$0
Tax on money market at 25% annually	$17,339	$17,339
Net usable cash	**$351,916**	**$446,103**

Almost halfway to being a millionaire. Not bad.

But what if you're already 50 years old and starting over, like I had to do? The book is entitled *100 Ways to Save and* Grow *Your Money,* so you'll have to focus on the *growth* ideas to bring in extra income. That will enable you to inject more money into compound interest and to grow your accounts faster. You can do it! Others— names you would recognize—have started right where you are, maybe with nothing or even worse, with incredibly high debt, at age 50 or 60. They still became financially independent in their lifetime. The power and magic is in *deciding* to do it, covering your plan with prayer and faith.

And then *doing* it.

11. Be consistent.

Here is one last look at what can happen with a solid interest rate and some discipline. Choose where you want to be at a point in the future, and work backward to find the amount you need to be saving monthly. If that number seems impossible now, don't get discouraged. Use the ideas in this book to save and grow your money until that monthly savings amount becomes a reality for you.

Monthly Savings	Total after 5 years at 8%	Total after 10 years at 8%	Total after 20 years at 8%	Total after 30 years at 8%	Total after 40 years at 8%
$10	$735	$1,829	$5,890	$14,904	$34,910
$50	$3,674	$9,147	$29,451	$74,518	$174,550
$100	$7,348	$18,295	$58,902	$149,036	$349,101
$500	$36,738	$91,473	$294,510	$745,180	$1,745,504
$1,000	$73,477	$182,946	$589,020	$1,490,359	$3,491,008

Just choose the goal you want, and *start now!*

"I [Wisdom] love those who love me, and those who seek me find me. With me are riches and honor, enduring wealth and prosperity." —Proverbs 8:17-18

NOTES

Bonus Section

TRAVEL AND ENTERTAINMENT

*"Finally, brothers, whatever is true, whatever is noble,
whatever is right, whatever is pure, whatever is lovely,
whatever is admirable— if anything is excellent or
praiseworthy— think about such things."*
—Philippians 4:8

*"Six days you shall labor, but on the seventh day you shall
rest; even during plowing season and harvest you must
rest."*
—Exodus 34:21

1. Free!

Now, lest you think that I am suggesting you work 24/7 on your financial goals, here is a bonus section with ten *more* ways to save money—all while you are taking a breather from all of your planning, working, and saving. You've already saved money, because you paid for 100 ways and received more than 110 ways! This first suggestion is to take that breather. Your mind and body will serve you so much better when you've had enough rest, exercise, and fun. And all three can be *free*.

2. Movies

If you like to go to the movies, consider this: a family of four at a first-run movie costs more than $50 for tickets, popcorn, and a drink. If you go even once a month, that's $600 a year. If you'll just change your "expecter" a little bit, you can see the same movies at the "dollar theater" a couple of months later for about one fourth the price. Or go only to matinees (these are usually in the morning or early afternoon), which have lower rates than the evening show times. Or wait for the movie to come out on DVD, and then rent it for $5.^{00} at your local video store.

The lowest cost we have found is Netflix, which mails DVDs to your house as fast as you return them. With this service, your movie costs drop close to a dollar each. At this writing, their cheapest plan is about $8 a month for as many movies as you want. If you watched a movie every time one arrived in your mailbox and dropped it back into the mail the next day, you'd see five to eight movies every month. That's less than $1.50 a movie, plus about a dollar for popcorn you bought at the grocery store. Maybe you'll spend $5.^{00} instead of $50.^{00} and see a lot more movies.

At this writing, Netflix also enables you to watch many of their catalog of movies, instantly, on-demand, at no extra charge. You can do this on your computer screen or using their internet interface box which connects to your TV. Amazing and basically free.

3. Professional sports

Similar to the movie section, this one can save you even more money by watching the game at home on TV or at your local sports restaurant that has a wide-screen TV. Season tickets are a lot of fun. But the grocery store won't take them in exchange for food, and your mortgage company won't take them in exchange for a mortgage payment, if you happen to lose your job. Until you have your debts paid down and at least six months' living expenses in the bank, don't be tempted to buy the top-level cable package to get all the professional sports games. This is a luxury, not a necessity. There are plenty of games to watch for free on the basic service. While paying down debt and saving for emergencies, we can live with low-cost analog cable or even an antenna on our roof to receive signals for free. You can save more than $50 a month or $600 a year by making this change.

4. Family fun

Do you have a Bocci ball set gathering dust in your closet or garage? What about those bicycles whose tires are flat from non-use? Maybe a couple of baseball gloves or tennis racquets that are getting lonely? What about those running shoes that ran to the closet a week after you bought them? You can get your exercise and enjoy time with your family for *free* by using what you already have. It might even be more fun than going to an event that costs money, and you'll talk to each other and enjoy each other's company more this way. One of the best things we ever did for our marriage was to begin taking walks together in the evening. Most evenings, we take a walk through our neighborhood and talk. It's *free,* and these times are some of the best we have had together. It might even save you some money on marriage counseling if you'll take the time to build your relationship like this. We did.

5. Music

There are several ways to save money on your music habit. First, you can find listening stations at some stores that allow you to hear part of each song on a CD. You might decide that you like only two songs on that CD. In that case, you can download just those two songs from a service like iTunes at www.apple.com for about a dollar each. This will save $16.^{00} to $18.^{00} over the cost of the full CD. In fact, you can hear part of each song on iTunes itself before deciding which songs to download. If you download two songs a week, you'll still save money compared to buying new CD's, but you'll still spend more than $100 a year on music.

If you are still paying down debt and don't have your minimum six to twelve months of living expenses saved, maybe that $100 could go to better use, like paying down a credit card or at least getting the payment to them soon enough to avoid a late fee. So listen to the radio—for *free*! Don't have a radio? Listen on your computer. Many stations have a streaming audio feed on the Web—for *free*. In fact, you'll find a lot more stations online than you can hear on your radio dial, because your computer can tap into music from all over the world—*free*. Some companies are now selling Internet radios, which get all of their music from the Web, cheaper than some computers. But if you already own a computer, use that. You don't have to spend money on an Internet radio. You can even connect your computer to your stereo tuner with a cable, and listen large. Here are some great, *free* music Web sites you may want to try: www.pandora.com and www.live365.com.

6. Surfing

Need to surf the Web for networking, entertainment, business, job searching, or education, but don't have a computer? You don't have to spend a thousand dollars to get online. At this writing, there are a lot of new "netbooks" coming onto the market—small laptops that sell for as little as $200 with Windows operating systems and full online capability. If you use the computer to download coupons you'll use at your grocery store, you can pay back the cost of your netbook pretty fast. Shop around for an ISP (Internet Service Provider) with decent speed and low rates, and be sure to read the fine print. We changed from our cable company's fastest service to the almost-slowest-service, and didn't notice much change in speed. But it saved about $20.^{00} every month or $240 a year. If you aren't a gamer or power user who needs the fastest thing out there, a netbook will save you $500 to $800 in purchase cost alone. Maybe you'll be able to buy it for cash and use the savings to pay down another debt.

You can also surf the Web free at your local library. It's less convenient than your kitchen table, but free is *free.*

7. Travel

Vacations are necessary for mental health; I am convinced of this. But if your vacation puts you in debt until the next one, it might actually increase your level of stress. Here are some ways to save money on your vacation:

- Book hotels through an online service, but only if it is better than the direct rate. Check the online rate at sites like www.travelocity.com or www.hotels.com and then call the hotel directly to make sure you are getting a good deal. Check the online services at different times during the month or two before your trip, as rates do fluctuate. These services also let you see photos inside and out, a lot of hotel rates compared to others, all the amenities, maps to their location, and reviews by travelers.

- The only thing better than a low rate is a free night. If you use the same hotel chain often, make sure to join their loyalty program. I recently stayed at an expensive hotel free by using loyalty points from business travel.

- Bring food with you. Food from your grocery store is almost always cheaper (and often healthier) than buying fast food or other restaurant food on the road.

- Drive instead of fly. Be careful here, as sometimes a flight may actually be cheaper, depending on the number of people traveling with you. When making this calculation, be sure to include the cost of getting to and from the airport and parking. For a family of four or five, it is almost always less expensive to drive. This also gives you time in the car together to enjoy each other's company (depending on family dynamics, this may be a good thing or not so good).

- If your family owns two cars, make sure to take the one with the best gas mileage on long trips (if you can all fit into it!).

- Download coupons and discount tickets for the area you are traveling to, and take them with you. Also bring maps and your GPS, if you have one, to shorten drive time to each event and save money on gas.

- Use the Web sites mentioned in Chapter 2 to find the lowest-cost gas all along your route and at your destination city. Do this ahead of time so that the info will already be with you when you need it.

- Stay with family. Doing so means less privacy, but maybe privacy is a luxury you don't need at this stage of your life. If staying with friends or relatives saves $500 to $1,000 in hotel bills and that enables you to pay off a credit card, it might be worth it (depending how well you get along with your in-laws).

- Whenever you check out of a hotel, bring the little shampoo, conditioner, and lotion that you already paid for. The next hotel might not have them, and buying these things at a convenience store on the road is almost always expensive. You can also use them at home or when camping, or to help you avoid buying travel-size toiletries for the next trip.

8. Timeshares

Never, ever buy a timeshare new from the developer. You'll pay two times to ten times the price you could get on the resale market, either through Ebay or through a timeshare agent online. A single timeshare week can cost between $10,000 and $30,000 or more, if bought from the developer or property manager. But you can buy those same timeshare weeks from an existing owner or third party for $2,000 or so. Beware: All timeshares come with annual maintenance fees and exchange service fees, all of which seem to come at the most inconvenient time, when some other bill is due.

It's generally less expensive to look for hotel deals. With a hotel, you can choose if and when to spend that money, if and when to travel. But with a timeshare, the maintenance fee is due every year, whether you are able to travel that year or not, and whether or not you need that money to pay for kid's braces, car repair, or credit payoff. If you do choose to invest in a timeshare, investigate thoroughly, and buy well. This means a high-quality property at a low price, usually purchased from someone who doesn't want theirs any more.

9. Las Vegas

A visit to Las Vegas can erase months (or even years) of diligent saving and growing of your money. The casinos are specially designed to separate you from your money. So choose a better plan—a different destination and a different activity. You'll have less stress and more money after your vacation by choosing a beach or a mountain or even an expensive theme park! Every casino, whether in Vegas or Atlantic City or anyplace else, was built and funded with the money of the losers. The casino doesn't lose, so guess who the losers are? Don't be one. The odds are in their favor, not yours. You have a better than average chance of leaving the casino with less money than you had when you arrived. Not a good investment.

You've heard it said that "what happens in Vegas stays in Vegas"? The only truth in that statement is all the money you will leave in Vegas when you go home.

10. The great outdoors

If you are adventurous and already have the equipment, you can camp at a campground or in the wilderness for far less money than staying at a hotel. Even if you don't have the equipment, you can purchase a tent and a few camping items for a few hundred dollars and use them for years of camping. You can stay in a developed campground such as KOA for $25.00 to $35.00 a night. Compare this to even the lowest-cost hotels. These developed campgrounds usually have rest rooms with showers, convenience stores, and even electric and water service. Or you can stay in a national forest—free. With some planning, you can also visit national parks, monuments, and natural landmarks, using your campground as a base—for free, or very low cost.

Our favorite vacations with our family have not involved amusement parks or any other particularly expensive activity; they have been the ones in which we played games, hit a few golf balls, played catch, and enjoyed seeing amazing things together. The same goes for family life at home; expensive video games, wide-screen TVs and other toys have not provided financial freedom or closer relationships. Someone once said the best things in life are free; I think it was someone who knew the truth. But use this *freeness* to build your family's wealth so that you can help others. There is an entire world of suffering fellow humans out there who need people of means to help them start a business, build an AIDS treatment center, repair a school, and feed the hungry. You can only help if you first become disciplined enough to build the wealth required to help them.

You can help—starting now, with as little as $10.^{00} to $25.^{00}—by giving in one of these ways:

- Sponsor a child through Compassion International at www.compassion.com

- Sponsor a child through World Vision at www.worldvision.org

- Lend to an entrepreneur in the developing world through Kiva at www.kiva.org

- Help break the cycle of extreme poverty by simply changing the way you buy certain products, www.tradeasone.com

- Help prevent the one out of four deaths worldwide that is caused by the lack of clean water. www.thewaterproject.com or www.adventconspiracy.org

- Sponsor a kid you know to raise funds through Hoops of Hope www.hoopsofhope.org, every penny of which goes directly to help HIV/AIDS orphans in Africa.

You can be practically destitute in the United States and still live better than 90 percent of the world's population. You have enough to help someone else, so get into the habit now. *"Whoever can be trusted with very little can also be trusted with much"* —Luke 16:10. Creating good giving habits now will result in massive benevolence once you have built your own family's wealth, and you will bless the world more than you can imagine today.

This book has helped you, yes?

Tell three friends about it! It will help them too.

NOTES

_____

_____

_____

_____

_____

_____

_____

_____

_____

_____

_____

_____

_____

SAMPLE MONTHLY BUDGET

Month and Year: Savings goal this month: Day of month:	1	2	3	4	5	6	7	8	9	10
Income:										
Wages/salary 1										
Wages/salary 2										
Home business										
Other										
Pay Yourself:										
Savings										
Fixed Expenses:										
Mortgage/rent										
Auto expense										
Loans										
Utilities										
Insurance										
Variable Expenses:										
Groceries										
Clothes										
Personal										
House expense										
Gifts										
Travel										
Entertainment										
Restaurant										
Miscellaneous										
Tax-deductible:										
Medical										
Contributions										
IRA/401K										
Daily Total										

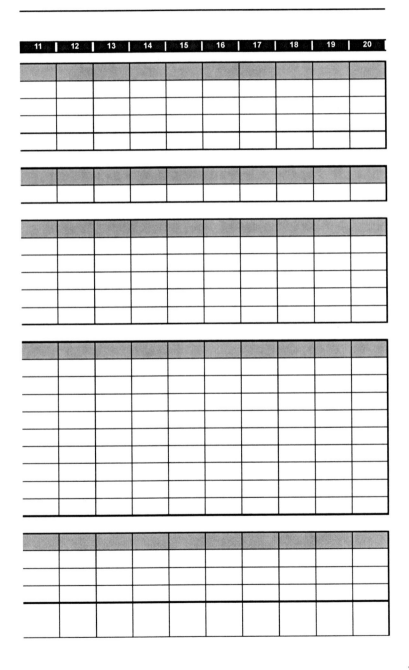

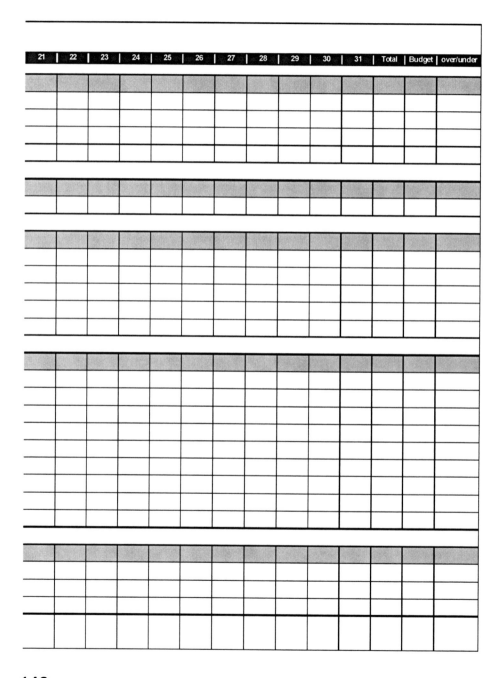

21	22	23	24	25	26	27	28	29	30	31	Total	Budget	over/under

Watch for these new products from Best Books, LLC:

CD Audiobook version of
100 Ways to Save and Grow *Your* Money:
Financial Fitness for Regular People

The Best Books Budget Book

Downloadable budget form in Excel format

Learn more at www.BestBooksLLC.com

For information about Best Books, LLC, or to report errors,
please e-mail: manager@BestBooksLLC.com

CPSIA information can be obtained at www.ICGtesting.com
Printed in the USA
BVOW010820250213

314028BV00006B/15/P

9 780984 341405